EVERYTHING YOU NEED TO
CREATE, RUN, AND PROFIT FROM
A MASTERMIND GROUP

MASTERMIND GROUP BLUEPRINT

TOBE BROCKNER

Mastermind Group Blueprint
Everything You Need to Create, Run, and Profit From
a Mastermind Group
By Tobe Brockner
Copyright ©2014 Tobe Brockner

For further information about speaking engagements, professional consultation, special bulk pricing, or other related inquiries, see the author's website at www.TobeBrockner.com.

Print ISBN: 978-1-61206-071-2
Library of Congress Control Number: 2013947555

Published by Aloha Publishing
AlohaPublishing.com

Printed in the United States of America

DEDICATION

When Ernest Hemingway said writing was easy and all you had to do to write was sit down at the typewriter and bleed, he wasn't kidding. Thankfully, I have surrounded myself with great people who encouraged me every step of the way and helped keep the blood flow to a minimum.

First, I would like to thank my wife, Kirsten. When we were $40,000 in debt, and I was making payroll with credit card checks, she still believed in me.

To my Aloha authors group, I appreciate your cheerleading and ideas on how to make this book better.

To Maryanna Young and Amy Larson, you two were instrumental in getting these ideas out of my head and onto paper in a coherent format. You are both talented ladies that I am proud to call friends.

And finally, to my Mastermind Group members, you inspire me; you teach me; and you humble me. I couldn't imagine a life where I didn't get to hang out with you each month and see the incredible things you are doing in your businesses. You all rock!

CONTENTS

CHAPTER 1:

THE POWER OF THE MASTERMIND GROUP

As a freshman in college, I visited my favorite bookstore one day between classes, full of that special kind of ambition you have when you are young and have your whole life in front of you.

I spent hours and hours dreaming of my perfect future, planning my life down to the minutest details. To help me on this quest, I turned to the one thing I always had when wanting to explore what life had to offer: books.

That particular afternoon I was in the self-help section, running my hand along the crisp spines of books on the shelves. As I perused the titles, my fingers came to rest on a book I had heard of before but had never read. I gently pulled Napoleon Hill's *Think and Grow Rich* from its place and opened it. Little did I know, that book would shape the rest of my life. Time and time again throughout my career, I returned to its words like an old friend, seeking advice and guidance.

I took the ideas and principles Hill outlined to heart. Over time, I tried to implement as many of them as I could into my own life, but there was one above all others that made the most impact: the principle of the Mastermind.

WHAT IS A MASTERMIND?

If you are not familiar with *Think and Grow Rich,* I need to give you a little background on Napoleon Hill and how this book came to be.

When Hill was just a young man, he went to see Andrew Carnegie, steel tycoon and arguably the richest man in America at that time. Napoleon Hill was obsessed with what made men like Carnegie so successful. He set out on a lifelong quest to find out if these men shared any common principles.

During his research, Napoleon Hill identified seventeen different principles like persistence, desire, faith, ambition, and, of course, the Mastermind principle.

To describe the Mastermind concept, let me give you a quick analogy. Let's say that you have an apple and I have an apple. If we trade apples, you still only have one apple and I still only have one apple. But, let's say that you and I both have an *idea*. If we exchange ideas, then you have two ideas and I have two ideas. That is, you have your original idea plus my idea, and I will have your idea plus my original idea.

If we add a third person into the mix, we each have three ideas, and so on. What is so powerful about this principle is that when two or more minds get together in a spirit of harmony and understanding, as Hill put it, then a third mind, a mastermind, is created.

Hill stumbled upon this particular principle while researching the life of Henry Ford. He found that Ford met formally with a group of men who did not work at Ford Motor Company at least once per month with the intent of sharing ideas, solving problems, and identifying opportunities.

Ford's original group consisted of Harvey Firestone, John Burroughs, Luther Burbank, and Thomas Edison. Quite the group of genius minds.

Undoubtedly, these are a few names that you recognize. Thomas Edison, of course, is one of our nation's most celebrated thinkers and inventors. Harvey Firestone is the founder of Firestone Tires, an obvious choice for Ford to include in his group. The other members, however, are not quite so obvious.

Naturalist and essayist John Burroughs was instrumental in the conservation movement. He was also a federal bank examiner for the Treasury Department. Close friends with Walt Whitman, Burroughs became a celebrated philosopher in his own right, publishing countless articles and essays on philosophy, nature, and literature.

Luther Burbank was a different sort of character. A botanist and horticulturist by trade, he was also an inventor of sorts. His inventions consisted mainly of different combinations of plants, fruits, flowers, grains, grasses, and vegetables.

In this eclectic group, Ford found solace, like minds, and inspiration. When asked about the secret of his success, he said on several occasions that his monthly group meetings with these four men were pivotal in helping him reach the heights to which he arose.

Ford spoke openly about how each member brought certain viewpoints and strengths to the group, strengths he himself did not possess. He acknowledged their contributions, expressing that, without their input, he could never have become the man who emerged. Powerful words from one of the most powerful men in our history.

Many times, when we are tending to the daily grind of our own particular businesses, we are sometimes blind to solutions that may seem obvious or intuitive to those on the outside looking in. By bringing others into our circle and presenting our various problems or opportunities, we are shown solutions we would never have seen on our own, and vice versa.

Personally, I have been brought into clients' businesses or have had business-owner friends ask for advice and have been able to present them with a solution to a problem or challenge that seemed obvious to me, but wasn't so obvious to them. In many cases, it was a two-way street.

Lest you are still not convinced of the power of the Mastermind Group, allow me to highlight the many benefits of participation. There are some obvious but also not-so-obvious benefits you should also consider. By the end of this chapter, you will be convinced—as am I and as was Henry Ford—that a Mastermind Group is an important key to your success.

WHY YOU SHOULD JOIN OR START A MASTERMIND GROUP

When I talk to people about starting or joining a Mastermind Group, the biggest reason they give for not joining is the time commitment. (Most Mastermind Groups meet monthly for *too busy driving your car around to stop for gas*

a minimum of four hours; a topic that will be covered in depth in a later chapter.)

To paraphrase the late Stephen Covey, that's like being too busy driving your car around to stop for gas. The pros of being in a Mastermind Group far outweigh any potential cons. Let me take a minute here to highlight some of those benefits.

THE ABILITY TO WORK "ON" YOUR BUSINESS INSTEAD OF JUST "IN" YOUR BUSINESS

When you get bogged down in the daily minutiae of your business, it can be difficult to see the bigger picture. Strategy and planning tend to take a backseat to solving daily problems or putting out those inevitable fires that pop up so regularly.

By joining a Mastermind Group, you have an opportunity, as Michael Gerber put it in *The E-Myth*, to work *on* your business and not just *in* it. That means you can dedicate time each month toward developing your strategy, planning your business's future, and making broader decisions that affect the direction, culture, and shape of your business. In short, it will give you the opportunity to design your business exactly the way you want it. The best part is that you'll have expert help.

CAMARADERIE AND UNDERSTANDING

I have long said entrepreneurs are some of the loneliest people on the planet. Most of us are surrounded by people relatively close to us but rarely by people who *understand* us.

We go to work every day solving problems, creating opportunities, and making things happen. There is really no one around whom we can confide in, lean on, or turn to for advice. We are expected to be the person who can be confided in, turned to, or asked for advice.

If you are anything like me, you revel in that. That attitude or character trait is what makes us entrepreneurs. I wouldn't trade it for the world, but it sure is nice to associate with others who experience the same challenges I do, who see things as I do, and who can identify with me.

That's what a Mastermind Group provides. Some of my closest friends have come from my association with various Mastermind Groups. I talk about my business with them in ways that I wouldn't dare in front of employees, vendors, or other non-business-owner friends. In many cases, non-Masterminds just wouldn't understand what I am going through. With these like-minded warriors in the trenches, I can be more open and frank. I know they are going to get me. That's a pleasant change from not being able to share defeats, triumphs, failures, and successes with anyone else in my world.

UNIQUE PERSPECTIVES

Not long ago, one of the Mastermind groups I moderate had a financial advisor put together what is called a "Shock 'n Awe" package to give to prospective clients and leads, so named because it was designed to do just that . . . shock and awe its recipients.

After explaining each piece of his package with the group members, a lady who runs an eldercare practice said, "You know, this is exactly the kind of thing I need to give to my prospective clients." We took the template the financial advisor showed us, and customized the different components into her own "Shock 'n Awe" package.

By taking an already developed idea and making a few tweaks and minor changes, this lady had a complete lead generation tool to turn her prospects into customers. This was something she may not have thought of on her own, and even if she had, it would have taken much more time and resources to develop it fully. Through her participation in the Mastermind group, she was able to glean the unique perspective of the other members, effectively shortcutting the creative process.

MOTIVATION

Let's face it; business isn't always fun and pleasant. Problems and challenges crop up on a daily basis that no one else in the world has to face the way we do. Staying motivated and inspired is a constant challenge.

When you surround yourself with business people who are excited, passionate, and energetic about the challenges they're presented with, you can't help but feel the same way.

That energy and passion rubs off, leaving you inspired and motivated. That's why it is so important to meet regularly with a group of like-minded people who feed your inner motivation. It's a way to recharge and reset each month, ready to face whatever comes your way.

ACCUMULATED EXPERIENCE

No two people will ever see the same events the same way. You and I could experience the same exact thing, and then come away with very different versions of what happened. That's why crime witnesses sometimes have such conflicting stories, viewing the occurrences very differently from each other.

Several business owners who have been in business for the same number of years can come up with spectacular solu-

the more you give, the more you receive

tions to problems, even if none of them have been in business very long. Their accumulated experience makes the difference.

Each year you are in business adds layers of experiences to your perspective. When you combine your knowledge with those of other business owners, you create a brand new perspective from which to work. It really goes back to the benefit of unique perspectives, but takes it a step further.

Not only do you benefit from the unique group perspective, you are also adding your own experiences to create a leveraged idea. This is extremely powerful, enabling you to solve problems or see ways to take advantage of opportunities. Don't underestimate that power.

ABILITY TO SERVE

I know it sounds cliché and it probably is, but it is still true: the more you give, the more you receive. It's one of those inexplicable realities of life. I would recommend not analyzing it to death or fighting it, but just going with and embracing it.

Joining or creating a Mastermind Group is a fantastic way to give back to other business owners in your community or circle of acquaintances. You might be joining a group to help run your business and grow profits, but you'll find that the quickest way to do this is to give of your time, talents, and ideas toward helping other group members grow their respective businesses.

Logically, taking that position makes sense. I mean, if everyone in the group has the attitude of being as much of service as possible, then it is natural that everyone benefits exponentially. Do your best to give as much as you can, and then watch the dividends of doing so pour into your own life.

ACCOUNTABILITY

I saved this benefit for last, because I absolutely believe that it is the single, most important reason for joining or starting a Mastermind Group. If none of the other benefits appeal to you, this one should.

Being an entrepreneur can be a lonely proposition; however, the other side of that coin is that you are essentially responsible for your own actions and for shaping your own future. In other words, you report to no one but yourself. There really is no one to hold you accountable for getting things done. That all changes once you join a Mastermind Group.

At one time I considered changing our meeting times from monthly to quarterly. When I presented this idea to the group, the overwhelming response was negative. As one of our members put it, "The only reason I get anything done in my business is because I come here every month and tell you guys what I am going to do during the next month. There's no way I would show up next month without getting those things done. I would be too embarrassed to show up and face you all."

There's something to be said about having a group like this to hold your feet to the fire and keep you accountable for getting things accomplished. It's much more difficult to push important tasks to the back burner when you know you'll be asked about them at the next Mastermind meeting.

The benefits of belonging to a Mastermind Group are substantial and can literally change your life and business for the better. If you are convinced that this could be true for you, then you are probably wondering what the requirements are for starting a group of your own or finding a group to join.

WHAT IS REQUIRED TO PARTICIPATE IN A MASTERMIND GROUP?

While there are no hard-and-fast rules regarding what is required to join a Mastermind Group, these are some general guidelines to use for your groups. Feel free to modify any of them in any way. There's no right or wrong answer here . . . just go with what will work for you.

MEMBERS FROM DIFFERENT INDUSTRIES

It is much easier to recruit potential members when limiting group membership to only one company per industry. Think about your own industry. If you were in a group with one or two of your biggest competitors, would you be as open when it comes to sharing ideas and strategies? Probably not. So, do your best to find members from different industries.

The flip side is that you will be masterminding with people who do not necessarily understand your business or industry. I have never really found that to be an issue. In fact, part of what makes a successful Mastermind Group is the unique viewpoints of the members.

COMMITMENT

For the group to be as effective as possible, individual members must be committed to it. If attendance is sporadic or inconsistent, there will be subpar results. Besides that, it's not really fair to other members if one or two don't attend regularly. The whole point is to have a collaboration of ideas. When people aren't there, collaboration suffers.

MEMBERSHIP DUES

One of the most effective ways to ensure group commitment is to charge membership dues. These can range from $25 up to $1,000 or more a month. There will be some costs involved in running a group such as food, beverages, handouts, printing costs, room rental, and marketing materials.

Apart from having the funds to pay for these items, there is also a psychological reason for charging dues.

If someone is paying to be a part of your group, he or she is much more likely to stick with it and take it seriously. I currently charge $297 per month for members to join our Mastermind Group, and members rarely miss a meeting. Charge whatever you want, but make sure it is enough to keep them committed.

You also want to consider the level of expertise you bring to the table as a moderator. If you aren't really giving any input and strictly moderating the group, then you will probably charge towards the lower end of the scale.

If, however, you are an expert in any particular facet of business and you are sharing that expertise with the group, then you want to charge a premium for that knowledge and experience.

SIMILAR SITUATIONS

Although you should only have one person per industry in your group, you should also make sure that everyone is relatively similar in where they are in their business's growth stage.

You don't want a member who has a fifty-million-dollar, twenty-year-old company partnered with a company that has been in business for three years and is barely making five hundred thousand dollars annually. The guy doing fifty million will probably feel like the other business has nothing to offer him, while the guy doing five hundred thousand might feel a little out of his league.

I would argue that both could benefit from being around one another ... the fifty-million-dollar company could learn to get back to its entrepreneurial roots by masterminding with the five-hundred-thousand-dollar company, and the five-hundred-thousand-dollar company could learn what it takes to get to fifty million. Unfortunately, most people won't see it that way.

OPTIMISM AND A POSITIVE ATTITUDE

It's okay to plan for worst-case scenarios and create alternative plans, should your Plan A not work out, but there is no room for the eternal pessimist. Find members who have a generally positive outlook on life and business.

The pessimists of the world are fairly easy to spot, and you need to be on the lookout for them within your group. This is the guy (or gal) who complains about every little detail, from the venue to the food to the topics being presented. This person will respond to feedback with, "Well the problem with that is ..." It's the person who is quick to shoot ideas down without giving any positive feedback or practical solutions to the problems presented. These behaviors are telltale signs that you have a bona fide pessimist on your hands.

Remember, one of the main benefits of the Mastermind Group is to be inspired and motivated by smart, sophisticated, passionate business owners. One bad apple can spoil the bunch, and nothing will make your group disintegrate faster than negativity. If you encounter a pessimist in your group, you will need to take quick action to rectify the situation. I recommend first having a frank discussion with that person. If things do not improve, you may have to ask them to leave the group.

ABSOLUTE DISCRETION

It is critically important that you instill a grave sense of discretion among your Mastermind members. This goes beyond the whole "What happens in Vegas stays in Vegas" concept.

Your members (and you) are going to be sharing intimately personal details about themselves, their employees, their competitors, their business practices, and their trade secrets. It is absolutely imperative that the group members treat this with the utmost respect and care. Trust is mandatory.

My Mastermind members are required to sign nondisclosure agreements that have stiff violation penalties. Fortunately, I have never had to use any of the penalties against anyone, but the simple fact that I take it so seriously with my members goes a long way in fostering a culture of openness and trust. I strongly suggest you do something similar.

As you can see, Mastermind Groups are a fabulous way to take your business to the next level, no matter where you are in your entrepreneurial journey. In the next chapter, we will get into the actual nuts and bolts of moderating a group.

CHAPTER 2:

BUT I CAN'T RUN A MASTERMIND MEETING!

You have learned about the benefits of being a part of a Mastermind Group. There's yet another benefit, and that is how little time it will actually take you each month to run a successful group.

On average, it shouldn't take more than a few hours *per month* to organize, plan, and host a monthly Mastermind Group. If it is extra money you are hoping to make, you will generate an extra $1,500 to $3,000 a month for just a few hours "work." Not too bad.

If you aren't motivated by the monetary rewards of running a Mastermind Group and are more interested in just growing your business, then this is a small but powerful investment you can make towards that goal.

You are going to explore exactly what you will need to successfully host a Mastermind Group. As you will see, it is fairly simple, but each component is important. These days, more than anything, consumers aren't just looking for extraordinary products or services. They are looking for extraordinary *experiences*. By following the guidelines listed below, you will have the tools necessary to create an experience your members will love.

There are no hard-and-fast rules. Read through the guidelines that follow, choosing the ones that are most applicable to your situation. Feel free to modify anything you feel doesn't support what you are trying to accomplish. The important thing is to get your group up and running without spending a lot of unnecessary time and energy just planning and preparing.

In no particular order, here are the items you will need to consider when forming a Mastermind Group.

GROUP SIZE

I run several different types of Mastermind Groups, so the number of members for each group may vary in size, depending on the purpose, time allotted for meetings, and the format.

BUT I CAN'T RUN A MASTERMIND MEETING!

For example, I run a presentation-based, monthly marketing meeting with very little engagement on the audience's part. It is more like sitting in a classroom in college than an open group. There are, on average, around fifty to sixty business owners in attendance, so a lot of participation or audience engagement would be impractical. The meeting is only two hours long, and we would never be able to accommodate everyone who had a comment or a question.

Another group I run is focused on copywriting. We talk mostly about the art and science of writing sales letters, creating landing pages, postcards, space ads, Google ads, and so on. That group is smaller—about twelve people—and the meetings run for about an hour and a half. There is much more interaction in this meeting, but it is mostly presentation based as well.

Finally, traditional Mastermind Groups consist of no more than six people, each from different industries. There is some presentation involved in this meeting, but it consists of mostly group interaction. For now, I encourage you to follow this traditional model for your group.

Concentrate on keeping your group to a total of around four to six members, including you. Keep in mind that you can set up as many of these groups as you want, depending on the kind of time commitment you can make. My colleagues in other areas of the country are running anywhere from five to eight Mastermind meetings at once.

If you have a dozen friends or colleagues you think might be interested in joining your group, just set up two different groups. You may even consider rotating them through the different groups every six to eight months to keep things fresh and interesting among members.

FOOD, REFRESHMENTS, AND CATERING CONSIDERATIONS

While it may sound silly to hear that this is one of the most important considerations you should make, I am being serious when I say that it is. If you ask people to shell out $300 to $1,000 a month to attend your Mastermind Group, then you need to make it a GREAT event. Catered food is virtually mandatory.

It's these little details that will make or break your success. The way you sell this thing to people is by making it an elite, exclusive club into which they are being invited. It's not something just anyone can join. There is a screening process and possibly a waiting list. Reality is perception. Every little component—*every little component*—has to be congruent with this positioning, including the food. Maybe even especially the food.

So, don't be cheap. Think back to the last event you attended that had unimpressive, or possibly horrible, food. Chances are it colored the whole event. I have been to upscale, supposedly elegant events catered by Panda Express. No disrespect to Panda Express, but that isn't exactly what you would call gourmet, and in that situation was completely incongruent with the type of event taking place. There's a time and a place for casual dining, but your Mastermind Group meeting is not one of those times or places.

I would recommend that you find a well-established caterer with an impeccable reputation. Ask around and find a few you can try out. Have the potential caterers put some sample dishes together and create a tasting menu for you. That way you can taste a variety of dishes from each, and then choose the one that fits your budget and satisfies your palate.

Speaking of budgets, I mentioned not being cheap. It is far better to pay a dollar or two more per person and get really high-quality meals than to skimp and be met with disappointment. That old saying, "You get what you pay for" will never be truer than in this case.

That being said, you should expect to pay between ten and fourteen dollars per person, depending on the dishes chosen and how many are being catered. Really, if someone is paying you $300 a month, springing for fourteen dollars for really great food is a pretty good trade off.

Along with the food, make sure you provide plenty of drinks. I usually buy a few types of soda, juices, teas, and then also have plenty of bottled water on hand. If your caterer doesn't provide them (most will, but make sure to ask), you may have to buy utensils, plates, and napkins.

ROOM RENTAL/VENUE OPTIONS

We hold monthly marketing meetings in a nearby university classroom. The layout is congruent with its purpose, which works out great for the presentation-based style meeting.

However, our traditional Mastermind Groups are held in a large conference room at a local credit union. The branch manager of this particular credit union comes to the monthly marketing meetings (for free), in exchange for use of the room. This saves a significant amount of money each month. If you can work out a similar trade, it would be worth it to investigate your options.

Venue layout is important to the overall flow of your meetings. For a smaller group (four to six members), a round-table-type layout tends to work well. You don't want members sitting in rows where some sit behind others. For high group interaction, a layout like that is highly inconvenient. Members should sit in a circle or half circle where everyone is facing inward, towards everyone else, making group discussion much easier.

Any large room free from distractions will work. If in a large conference room, make sure you can close the doors to limit the amount of noise and distractions. In one group I was a part of, the conference room walls were made of glass, and you could see the outer offices. It was extremely distracting to see people walking by and chatting with one another.

You shouldn't be paying more than a couple of hundred dollars to rent a venue for these meetings, especially since you are using it for just a few hours each month. If you are being charged for the room you want to use, try to work out some sort of trade with the owner to limit your costs.

Other options for meeting rooms are hotel conference rooms, universities, public libraries, corporate offices, or executive suites. (Executive suites often provide a large conference room to its tenants, and these can sometimes be rented for less than one hundred dollars.) Look into various options, and you should be able to find an acceptable venue without too much trouble.

MEETING FORMAT AND LENGTH

I am going to assume you are reading this because you are interested in setting up a traditional Mastermind Group consisting of four to six members, from several different industries. If this is the case, I have a suggested meeting format and time frame for you to consider. Again, this is how I do it, but it is by no means the only way. In fact, you may start your group with these guidelines and then evolve your group format over time to accommodate your business and your members' particular needs.

Currently, I run my traditional Mastermind meetings for four hours, starting at 9 a.m. and going until 1 p.m. on a Friday. I have found that Fridays are the best days to hold a meeting because they are generally a light work day, and many of the daily tasks of a business are wrapped up before that time frame.

Around noon, the food arrives and we eat together as a group. Though these are all experienced business owners, there is always a teaching portion. Usually, but not always, it centers on marketing or revenue generation strategies. This is mainly because my background and expertise are in marketing and advertising and because I sincerely believe marketing is the single, most important function of any business.

Depending on how many people are in the group, I will go over a marketing topic for the first thirty to forty-five minutes of the meeting. We then take a quick restroom break and start with the first group member. That group member then has about forty-five minutes to talk about three or four challenges they are having in their business. The whole group participates in making suggestions, giving ideas, or fleshing out concepts related to the particular challenges under discussion.

Someone, usually my assistant, will take notes of the interaction and create checklists, to-do lists, and action items for that member to complete during the next month. This gives that member something tangible to take home and implement in business during the next thirty days. These meetings are not just about theory or ideas. They are about action.

After the first member is finished, we move on to the second person and the cycle repeats itself. During each member's allotted time, the other group members are busily taking notes themselves, analyzing the ideas that are flowing to see if they apply to their own businesses. A lot of the real growth in the group comes from hearing about a successful strategy in one business or industry and then applying it to another business or industry, with only minor modifications. In this way, we all get to have a chance at shortcutting the learning curve, and more importantly, we get to implement something in our own businesses that has already been proven in another business.

At the end of each meeting, I will usually take five to ten minutes to leave the group with a motivational or inspirational thought. This ends the meeting on a positive note and gets everyone excited to get back to work and start implementing their ideas through the next month until we meet again.

GROUND RULES FOR THE MEETING

Critical commitment to the group is necessary to instill this sense of commitment to potential group members as soon as possible. Every new member receives a copy of a welcome letter (a letter welcoming him or her to the group and providing the necessary contact information to get in touch with me), a copy of the nondisclosure agreement (which must be signed and turned in before the meeting starts), and a copy of the ground rules (which I will cover here).

ATTEND EVERY MEETING

I am pretty firm about this one. If you can't make a meeting, then you need to have a very good excuse. It's just not fair to the rest of the group (or to you) to miss a meeting. I have actually instituted a "Two Strikes, You're Out" policy, where if you miss two meetings during a calendar year, then you are gone. I've only had to enforce it once, but I think that by respecting this rule and ousting the offender, I showed the group I was serious about their commitment and respectful of their time and dedication.

Use your discretion when enforcing this rule (i.e., you may give someone a pass for a legitimate emergency), but just remember that this is about maintaining the integrity of the group and respecting everyone's time.

STAY FOR THE WHOLE MEETING

I had a guy in one of our Mastermind Groups stay long enough at the meeting to take his turn, then try to leave to "attend a client meeting." It was incredibly disrespectful to other group members and incredibly selfish as well.

The group is only as strong as the members' willingness to give to one another.

I had a discussion with him about it, and it never happened again, but this is also one policy where you really have to be firm.

SILENCE/TURN OFF CELL PHONES

This is the one place where you give yourself permission not to be at the mercy of the daily distractions that plague you. The group needs everyone's full attention, so turning off cell phones is a must. There are few business emergencies that can't wait a few hours until the meeting is over. I know some things seem like they are life and death, but trust me, they're not. Turn off your phone.

ACTIVELY PARTICIPATE

Nothing drives me crazier during these meetings than when members don't offer any suggestions or ideas. If members just sit there without offering anything to the group, I will usually try to gently draw them into the discussion with a friendly, "Well we've heard from everyone so far except for you, Jack. What do you think about this problem?" Then I will sit in silence with a smile on my face until Jack starts talking.

Usually that is all it takes. If you can get Jack talking—even just a little bit—you will find that the ice breaks, and he will begin to contribute to the discussion without any more prodding. Do your best to get everyone to participate, and make it a ground rule that they do so.

CONSTRUCTIVE CRITICISM ONLY/BE POSITIVE

Now, this isn't to say you can't talk about worst-case scenarios or plan for potential disasters, but one of the main purposes of this group is to find a source of motivation and inspiration. If there is a lot of negativity in the room, then it will to be difficult to find.

Any criticism should be expressed with tact and a sincere desire to provide a solid solution to problems or challenges being discussed. I don't believe that there are any inherently dumb ideas. There are only ideas that serve as the impetus for a goal-oriented discussion.

If you view all ideas as a starting point, you can then focus on building upon that original foundation until you have built that idea into something practical and useful for implementation.

Keep a positive outlook and remember why you are all there: to build one another up.

DON'T INTERRUPT ONE ANOTHER

When you get a bunch of Type A personalities, entrepreneurs, and business owners in a room together, it is natural that the egos involved will expand somewhat. After all, we are used to being the ones who provide the best solutions to the myriad of challenges and problems we face every day.

We have to remember none of us has the corner on the market of good ideas, and we all have valid and substantial ideas to present. So, we have to be mindful we are not interrupting or talking over one another, and everyone has a fair chance to speak their mind. Nothing ruins the free flow of ideas more than a bunch of people trying to talk over each other. As the moderator, it is your job to circumvent this, should it happen.

KEEP YOUR COMMENTS CONCISE. DON'T BE A TIME HOG.

Talking for long stretches of time without allowing anyone else to participate or get a word in edgewise makes you a time hog. Not only will you stifle open discussion, you will also suffer resentment from the group. Keep it short and sweet. Be of value, but not long winded. If someone in the group is going on and on, it is your responsibility to gently interrupt and refocus the discussion, drawing other members into the conversation.

These are basic ground rules, and you may think of others that will be necessary. Keep tweaking things until you find that perfect balance.

MISCELLANEOUS ITEMS

You have covered the main points of what you'll need to run a meeting, but there are a ton of little items you will also need that you may not have thought of. The following probably isn't a complete list, but here are a few additional items you'll want to consider:

- Cooler (for the beverages)

- Pens and/or notepads (in case someone forgets to bring one)

- Digital recorder (If you want to record your meetings and give your members audio CDs of them; offering a recording of the meeting adds lots of value and makes a big impression!)

- Computer/laptop

- Whiteboard with markers and eraser

- Separate business entity and bank account (so as not to comingle funds with your main business funds)

- Merchant account (to take credit cards, separate from your main business account)

- Timer, clock, or stopwatch (to keep track of how long each person gets to speak)

Obviously, none of these items are required but might come in handy when conducting an efficient meeting.

Running a Mastermind meeting is a fairly simple process, but someone needs to attend to the little details described in this chapter to make sure it all runs smoothly. If you take these suggestions to heart, I have full confidence you will be able to run a Mastermind Group your members will appreciate and enjoy.

In the next chapter, you will learn about the teaching portion of the meeting and where you will discover exactly what types of information and presentations you should offer your group each month.

CHAPTER 3:

WHAT AM I SUPPOSED TO TALK ABOUT ANYWAY?

Now that you have the mechanical logistics of a meeting down, you will need to come up with content to present during each monthly meeting. A basic meeting agenda will look like this:

9:00 a.m.–9:45 a.m.	Presentation to Group
9:45 a.m.–9:50 a.m.	Break
9:50 a.m.–10:30 a.m.	Member 1 Speaks
10:30 a.m.–11:10 a.m.	Member 2 Speaks
11:10 a.m.–11:15 a.m.	Break
11:15 a.m.–11:55 a.m.	Member 3 Speaks
11:55 a.m.–12:05 p.m.	Lunch
12:05 p.m.–12:45 p.m.	Member 4 Speaks
12:45 p.m.–1:00 p.m.	Wrap Up/Q&A/Etc.

teaching portion ① be the expert ② client expectation

This agenda assumes you have at least four members in your group. The times will have to be adjusted if there are more or fewer members. Other factors may be considered. For example, this agenda provides forty-five minutes of your own presentation time, and then each member gets forty minutes to work on his or her business. You could make your presentation time only twenty-five minutes long and give each member forty-five minutes to work with. It's up to you.

Friends of mine who also run Mastermind Groups in their cities don't have a teaching portion at all. They just dive right into everyone's business and start throwing out ideas. I like to offer a teaching portion for two primary reasons.

First, if I am teaching the group something of value, then it further establishes me as an expert and authority on the subject matter. Since I view my group members as clients, this is important to me. The educational factor also serves to retain them as members for much longer.

Not only are they getting to work on their business every month, they are also learning valuable, practical strategies to implement in that business.

Second, I find that teaching a principle or concept at the beginning of the meeting serves as a way to get creative juices flowing. It helps to mentally pull members into the meeting, preparing their brains to start thinking creatively. If you

3 categories of content mindset, strategy, tactics

have ever "primed the pump," so to speak, you will find ideas coming to you much more readily than if you had just started cold. This way whoever goes first gets the same benefit of a warmed-up crowd as the guy who goes last. Everyone is more productive.

What exactly do you talk about during this presentation time? And what should your group members be talking about during their own allotted time? Those are the two questions we are going to answer in this chapter.

PRESENTATION CONTENT FOR MEMBERS

There are three main categories here that you can choose from. I would recommend that you maintain a good balance between the three. You could alternate between the categories by presenting one category every third month, or figure out some other kind of schedule that works for your group. The main thing is that each category is important and should be presented to your group members.

The three categories are mindset, strategy, and tactics. Since you'll probably be rotating these categories out once every quarter, I'll give four examples per category that you can use for presentations. By the time you are done with this chapter, you will have enough presentation ideas to take you through a full year of Mastermind meetings. Let's cover each one in turn.

CATEGORY #1 – MINDSET

Mindset skills are what are often called "soft" skills. It's how you think, who you are, or who you want to be. These skills are intangible and difficult to quantify, but they are extremely important. Without a proper mindset, it will be extremely difficult, if not impossible, to create and design the business you envision.

There are literally hundreds, if not thousands, of topics you could discuss during Mastermind meetings, but I am going to cover four of the most important, although I am fully aware that "important" is a relative term. As you better get to know the members and the challenges they are facing, you will be able to choose topics that best address those needs. For now, here are four major mindset concepts you can present to your members.

Developing an Accurate Self-Image *I dentity*

I first studied this concept in a book written by Dr. Maxwell Maltz, a plastic surgeon, called *Psycho-Cybernetics* in the late 1960s. What he discovered was that people who came to him for surgery were sometimes not satisfied with their appearance, even after extensive reconstructive surgery had been done.

This led Dr. Maltz to the conclusion they weren't necessarily as unhappy with their outer image as they were with their inner or self-image. It was the way they thought about themselves that mattered. He wrote of people who were told their whole lives they weren't good at a particular skill, and so they never even tried to develop that skill. Their own defective self-image kept them from realizing their true potential.

The ability to see ourselves in a true light, not short changing ourselves based on preconceived notions or definitions others have labeled us with, is a crucial key to success.

Helping your members develop an accurate self-image is paramount to their overall business success. As Henry Ford once said, "Whether you think you can or you can't, you're right."

If this subject is interesting to you at all, I would highly recommend picking up a copy of Dr. Maltz's book.

Live Life on Purpose *Meaning & Purpose of life*

Related to the first topic, "Developing an Accurate Self-Image" is the idea of "Living Your Life on Purpose." In his book and companion DVD, *The Shift*, Dr. Wayne Dyer talked about creating a shift in your life from Ambition to Meaning. He argued when you begin your professional career, you have this idealistic vision of how your life should be that is usually based on others' view of what constitutes "success." This vision is the impetus for a burning ambition to succeed.

Since your view is blurred by what others have defined as successful, you find later in life you have reached all of your goals and are still left unfilled, unhappy. You realize the missing piece of the life puzzle is a life full of meaning. So, you begin to set goals that have personal meaning or purpose. As you let go of your ego and surrender to life, you find you are happier and feel more fulfilled. This is truly what freedom is all about. You are now living your life on purpose. It doesn't mean that you have no more ambition . . . it's just ambition with a purpose.

A big part of what you are offering your group members is inspiration. You are motivating them to become the best possible human beings they can be—to be contributors to their community, their families, and their economy. If you can show them how to be happy while doing that, you will have done your job properly. Make sure you get yourself a copy of the *The Shift* DVD and watch it. Take lots of notes.

Use the Power of Positive Thinking *See potential in others*

I know, I know . . . this one has been beaten to death. Yet it's still important and useful, especially in business, when there are so many things to be negative about. Lazy employees, rising costs, impossible financing terms, more government regulation and interference—it's a never ending stream of "stuff" trying to knock us down. That's why this topic is virtually mandatory.

thinking ⟷ doing ⟷ be

We have to develop the skills necessary to insulate ourselves from the external factors that would bring us down. Believe me when I say this type of presentation will be welcomed and embraced by your group members. They constantly have to be the ones spreading good cheer and optimism to those around them. It will be a nice change for them to be able to hear it from you and learn ways on how to better cope.

The authoritative resource on this topic is Norman Vincent Peale's *The Power of Positive Thinking*. If you have never read it, you are doing yourself a disservice. Grab a copy today and study it thoroughly.

If you do choose this topic, make sure to include some time around the idea of not just positive thinking, but positive *doing*. Too often you are taught that all you have to do is think positively and good things will happen. The real world, unfortunately, doesn't always work that way. It is up to you to make positive things happen, not just hope they will or feel entitled they will because you are thinking positive thoughts. That's naïve and dangerous. Your Mastermind members need a good dose of both concepts.

Staying Passionate about Your Business *Underneath infinite value and potential*

There's an old saying among start-up veterans that goes something like this, "When you first start your company, you have a lot of passion but very little knowledge. A year later you have lots of knowledge and no more passion."

I think that is true for most of us. That's one reason attending a monthly Mastermind Group is so important. So you don't let that fire of passion burn out. The good news is there are strategies you can implement to actually trigger passion. Not just for your business, but for your life, products, services, or other areas that need a good shot of passion injected into it.

One of the most qualified authorities on triggering passion in your business is Sally Hogshead, who wrote an excellent book called *Fascinate*. The book describes seven ways to create fascination for yourself, your business, or your products/ services. One of the seven is the concept of passion.

Sally said, "Passion for something means we crave it. This trigger can focus on an object, experience, or person; it might last moments, or a lifetime; yet in every case, passion captivates our desire for sensory fulfillment."

What a great way to wake up and feel about your business every day! I personally love this topic because of the excitement and energy it creates in my life when I talk about it and get others engaged. Try it out with your members and feel the passion and energy it creates.

Those are the four mindset presentations to start with. Pick up the recommended reading materials, study them, and you will be good to go. Next, we'll cover the strategy topics you can present.

CATEGORY #2 – STRATEGY DEVELOPMENT

We all have strengths and weaknesses and are good about strategizing on some things and poor at strategizing about others. A great thing about being in a Mastermind Group is being able to create strategies. Others can help you see the big picture, point out holes in your plans, and give objective feedback to make sure your strategies are sound.

Just as with the mindset section, there are a lot of things you could talk about here. The following strategies will be pertinent to any entrepreneur, regardless of what business he or she is in.

Marketing Strategy

I may be a little biased, but I am sincere when I say that marketing is the single, most important function in *any* business. Well-developed marketing plans are always in de-mand because, frankly, most business owners may be really talented at what they do in their business, but really suck at marketing.

There are two main things you need to develop a solid marketing strategy, both of which I will cover more in the discussion on Tactics. They are (1) incorporating a multimedia, multistep approach to your plan and (2) implementing aggressive follow-up to convert the leads that are generated.

First, most marketing nowadays fails not because the marketing piece or message/offer is bad, but because most business owners treat marketing as a one-time event instead of a process. They may send out a cheap postcard with an offer on it. When the response isn't overwhelming, they give up and claim, "Oh, direct mail doesn't work." In reality, they should have mailed the postcard, then a few days later another postcard, then a week later a sales letter, and then a few days later followed up with a phone call or e-mail. They should have multiple steps involved and use a variety of media, i.e. postcards, sales letters, phone calls, e-mail, etc.

Second, once a lead is generated—someone has expressed interest in their product or service—then business owners need a strategy for aggressively following up with that person until they buy, die, or tell them to go pound sand. Most business owners give up way too soon on leads who don't buy their goods or services immediately. That is shortsighted and leaves a lot of money on the table. When helping your group members develop their marketing strategy, that's where you'll start. If you need a resource to help you, I recommend *No B.S. Direct Marketing for Non-Direct Marketing Businesses* by Dan Kennedy. (Actually, while we're on the subject, I recommend reading anything and everything you can that Dan Kennedy has written.)

Financial Planning

This topic can be used in two ways, and I suggest covering both if possible and if your group is open to it. The first way is on the personal finance side and the second is on the business planning side.

The main reason for owning a business, regardless of what the government or society tries to tell you, is to take money out for your benefit. Not to provide jobs for employees, not to pay taxes, and not for any other reason other than for your benefit, and for the benefit of any shareholders you may have.

Strategizing about how to take the most money out of your business is an excellent topic to cover. If you aren't comfortable with trying to speak intelligently about this subject, you can always bring in experts to present to your group. Usually they will do it for free, since they could build a relationship with your members that could lead to a business relationship.

Once money has been taken out of the business, it needs to be protected and it needs to grow. This is where personal financial planning comes into play. There are a lot of viable strategies for accomplishing this, and I recommend that you cover several different strategies ranging by degrees of risk. Again, if this isn't in your area of expertise do not hesitate to bring an expert in to cover this topic.

Business Growth Strategies

When you talk about growing your business, most people jump to the conclusion that you are talking about growing revenue. While that is certainly a good topic to cover, it is by no means the only growth strategy available.

One area of growth that affects lots of businesses is making the decision on when, or if, to hire additional employees. Since labor costs are usually the highest expense a business has, thinking strategically about this challenge is important.

Another growth area ripe for discussion is how to grow the profits of a business, which doesn't necessarily translate into growing revenue. Bigger isn't always better, and higher gross doesn't always mean higher net. I'm reminded of the story about one business owner who exclaimed to a consultant, "We've got all this gross revenue. There has to be some net around here somewhere."

Growth in profits mostly has to do with cutting costs, creating efficiencies where none exist, and taking advantage of opportunity. These are all fantastic strategy discussions to have and are all areas where the collective "mastermind" of the group can be enormously beneficial, finding unique and creative ways to deal with these challenges and opportunities.

One last growth item is the introduction of new products or services. It can be a lot of fun (not to mention profitable) to figure out new things to offer your existing customers, or even tap brand new markets that present unique opportunities and congruencies with your existing products or services.

Referral Strategy

Every business on the planet can benefit from a well-developed referral strategy. When I ask potential clients in our initial consulting meeting where the majority of their customers come from, the answer I get most often is from referrals or word of mouth. However, when I dig a little deeper to see the plan they have in place for generating those referrals and that word of mouth, I am rarely given anything other than a blank stare.

I can go into almost any business and bump their revenue by 10 to 15 percent within sixty days, just by putting a well-thought-out referral strategy in place. If you need a place to start for developing a winning referral strategy, pick up a copy of John Jantsch's book *The Referral Engine* or Andy Sernovitz's *Word of Mouth Marketing*. Both are excellent resources.

This continues one of the main benefits of brainstorming with other sharp thinkers, which is developing solid business strategies for your company. Start with these four and you can't go wrong.

CATEGORY #3 – TACTICAL SKILLS

As important as strategy is, it is useless without the ability to execute those plans. In this section I will cover four tactical skills that come up over and over again that most business owners lack. These are the in-the-trenches, get-your-hands-dirty skills you need in order to survive the day-to-day battles on the business minefield.

Although I believe you can hire for virtually any skill, I also believe there are some skills, like the ones listed below, that every business owner should be adept at or at least knowledgeable about if they want to reach the pinnacle of success in their industry.

Communication Skills

Most business owners I know, at least among my clients, are type A personalities. They're assertive, somewhat aggressive, take-charge kind of people, men and women alike. This isn't to say they are mean (although the situation will often dictate whether they are or not), but that they are used to being in charge and making decisions.

These people know how they want things, and can often clearly see how things should be in their head. Many times, unfairly perhaps, they expect their subordinates to understand *exactly* what they want with very little explanation. I confess I am the same way. In fact, I had an employee say to me once, "It's like you expect me to be able to read your mind." And at the time I thought, "Yes. Yes, that's exactly what I expect."

It kind of goes without saying; we aren't all the best communicators. Communication, however, is a crucial skill. To be able to communicate effectively is the difference between things being done right or things getting screwed up. Make no mistake; the majority of the time, when things get screwed up, it's *our fault* for not being clear in our instructions and expectations. Fortunately, these are skills that can be learned fairly easily with willingness and just a little bit of effort. There are many great resources on how to communicate better, but a really practical book on the subject is *How to Communicate* by Matthew McKay.

Selling Skills

In the beginning of a business's life cycle, the best (and sometimes only) salesman is the business owner. Many of your group members may already be skilled in this area, but it never hurts to review. It really is that important.

Selling has undergone a transformation over the last ten to fifteen years, as new ideas and concepts replace old school methods. This evolution needs to be addressed with your Mastermind Group members so that they are up-to-date with the latest cutting edge tactics being used in today's selling environment.

There are two great books available that I recommend you get and study, both written by Dan Kennedy. The first one is called *No B.S. Sales Success in the New Economy* and the second one is titled *No B.S. Trust-Based Marketing*. I know the second says in the title it is about marketing, but trust me, it also has a great deal to do with selling.

Copywriting

If selling is the art and science of persuasion in person, then copywriting is the art and science of selling through media. Print, television, radio, direct mail, web pages—if it is sold by the written word then this is the skill of copywriting.

Being great at copywriting is one of the most underestimated skills business owners acquire, but it is extremely useful. The ability to sell through the written word is the single best way to leverage your time and resources and get the biggest bang for your marketing buck.

Even if your group members plan to outsource this function to a professional copywriter, it is still a skill worth honing if only to know what good copy looks like. By understanding what makes good copy, you will be in a much better position to critique your copywriter's work and turn out a winning ad or piece of sales copy.

Negotiating

Negotiating comes in many forms—with clients, with vendors, with government officials, with employees. It is a great skill to have for this myriad of circumstances.

Negotiating is somewhat similar to selling, as it has undergone a transformational shift in recent years. What was once considered gospel is now outdated and behind the times. Ironically, one of the best books I have read about negotiating is *The Go-Giver* by Bob Burg and John David Mann. Although technically a "sales book," the lessons contained within can apply to virtually any negotiating situation.

These are just a handful of tactical skills your Mastermind members should find useful. Start with these four and add any additional skill sets you feel will benefit your particular group the most. If you have any doubts, you can always ask your group members for ideas. They will tell you several areas where they feel additional training would be beneficial.

WHAT SHOULD YOUR GROUP MEMBERS TALK ABOUT DURING THEIR ALLOTTED TIME?

We have covered what you should be presenting during the first half hour to forty-five minutes of each meeting, but what about when it's time for your group members to get up and talk? What exactly should they be talking about?

The short answer is "whatever they want." Especially if they are paying to be there, they should feel free to use this time however they please. In the event they need a little guidance to get started, ask them to come prepared with three challenges or opportunities they are facing right now. This could be in any area of their business: finance, marketing, processes, systems, employee relations, vendor relations, revenue opportunities, new product/service development . . . the list goes on and on. If they come with three specific things, that should be enough to get everyone talking about solutions to those challenges or opportunities.

If you feel somewhat overwhelmed or even intimidated with the idea of teaching your Mastermind Group members any of the above topics, I have two things for you to keep in mind at all times.

First, remember the saying, "The one-eyed man is king in the land of the blind." If you study your topics even just a little bit, you will most likely know as much, if not more, than your audience.

Second, you are not so much a teacher as a moderator. That means you are simply guiding the discussion based on a structure you have put together. Encourage group participation by preparing a series of questions to throw out at to the group. Ask a question, then sit back and let them hash it out amongst themselves. Chances are you will be dealing with some pretty sharp people anyway, and they will create fascinating discussions with little to no input on your part.

Don't worry about feeling inadequate or ill prepared. This is as much about learning for you as it is for them. In the next chapter we are going to cover my favorite part: how to get new members through marketing. This is probably the most important chapter of this book. You can be a great presenter and run a killer meeting, but it's all a waste if you don't have any members.

CHAPTER 4:

MARKETING YOUR MASTERMIND GROUP: HOW AND WHERE TO GET NEW MEMBERS

Now that you have learned how to set up and run a meeting, your next immediate task is to fill it with members. None of this newly acquired knowledge will do you any good if you don't have people to share it with.

One of the biggest mistakes I made when I started my business career was thinking that marketing was a linear process: Step 1, Step 2, Step 3. Nothing could be further from the truth. It's not sequential as much as it is simultaneous. You have to do many things at the same time for the best results. There's an old adage in marketing I really like that goes something like this,

> *"I don't know of one way to get ten new customers, but I do know of ten ways to get one new customer and I use them all."*

I don't know that you will need ten different ways to get new members, but you'll at least need a handful. I will show you exactly what I do to attract new members and highlight marketing strategies that have been the most cost efficient and effective.

THE LEAD GENERATION PROCESS

I am going to assume that you will start your marketing efforts by inviting your own circle of colleagues and business acquaintances to attend your Mastermind Group. These are people you know and have some semblance of a relationship with who also know, like, and trust you. This is the proverbial "low-hanging fruit." (And don't worry; if you don't know how to approach them or what info to give them to explain what you are doing, we are going to talk about that in just a second.)

After you have exhausted your own contact list and would like to generate additional interest in your group(s), you will need a systematic way to identify potential members, find them, attract them, and convert them.

Marketing generally isn't sequential, but here is a basic process you can follow: identify, find, attract, and convert. If you follow and implement each of the various components in a consistent way, you will have a waiting list of eager prospects ready to join your group.

IDENTIFY YOUR POTENTIAL MEMBERS

It may seem logical that virtually every small business owner is a potential Mastermind Group member, but they are not. There are some very distinct characteristics that will set apart your potential members from run-of-the-mill business owners.

The biggest thing you want to look for are business owners who read a lot of self-help books, business books, and any other nonfiction works designed to help them improve their lives or business. This includes the purchase of home study courses, audio CDs, and DVD programs.

The second character trait you want to look for in a business owner is aggressive marketing. These entrepreneurs are the ones actively and aggressively trying to grow their business and aren't afraid of spending money to do it.

Finally, you want to find those business owners who are somewhat established. Entrepreneurs involved with very young companies or startups are pinching every penny and may balk at spending money to join your group, even if it will benefit them. Established business owners are more likely to see the value in joining a Mastermind Group. (If you are interested in working with start-up companies, you could start a Mastermind Group dedicated just for this purpose.)

This is the basic profile you want to keep in mind when getting your marketing plan together. To sum it up: you want a business owner who is interested in improving themselves and/or their business, is aggressive with their marketing, and has an established business.

FIND THEM

Once you have identified your ideal Mastermind Group member, you now need to find them. This isn't going to be as easy as it sounds, but I'll give you several ideas to start with.

Referrals:

This is the best place to begin your efforts. Keep in mind that like attracts like. In other words, we tend to associate with and attract those who are similar to us. Even if you only have a few Mastermind members right now, you'll want to start by getting them to refer their friends and colleagues to you.

Chances are, they are friends with and can positively influence potential members who would be a great fit for your group. Make sure your referral partners know the basic criteria we identified above, so that you will have the highest-quality prospects coming your way. You don't want to be snobbish about it, but a simple, "I've found that most of our Mastermind members are really into improving themselves and their business, are pretty aggressive with their marketing, and have been in business for a while. Do you know anyone else like that who would like to check out our group?"

If they say yes, then give them a packet of information to pass along to their friend or colleague who will do most of the "selling" of the group for you. In the next section we cover exactly what goes into this packet, but it's important to make referring people to you as easy for your members as possible.

Direct Mail:

I know, direct mail is dead, but hear me out. Your prospects are aggressive marketers. A successful approach is to mine the direct mail from local businesses, pull out the coupons in the Val-Pak and Money Mailer coupon decks, check the Yellow Pages for full-page ads, check the local billboards and bus bench ads, and basically try to capture the business name and address of any business that is being aggressive with their advertising.

Enter that information into your customer relationship management (CRM) database, creating a series of unique mailers that go out to these businesses over a sixty-day period. Currently, I send six mailers, about one every ten days. These aren't just ordinary sales letters. The very first one that goes out is a giant golden ticket with a letter taped to the front. The letter is simple, mentioning that I saw their ad, was impressed with their marketing, and then I tell them about our Mastermind Group and invite them to request a free info kit.

There were some raised eyebrows at the post office when I brought these in to mail, but they were mailed out just fine. Think about it…if you got a giant golden ticket in the mail, you would open that thing out of sheer curiosity to see who and why someone is mailing you something like that. After the golden ticket, follow up with another five letters or so, each referring to the previous letters. Urge them to request your free information and free complimentary ticket to attend a Mastermind meeting to see if they could benefit.

Website:

Although this is a business you can run in your spare time, it is still a business and requires a website. The website doesn't have to be fancy, but it does need to have a couple of important items. First, it needs an opt-in form where visitors can request additional information in exchange for their contact information. This is crucial. You need a way to capture contact information.

Second, the website needs to give enough information in such a way that visitors are compelled to learn more. If you don't know how to write sales copy, you might consider hiring this function out to a professional. It will be worth every penny and will make the difference between visitors hitting your site and leaving or staying and becoming an interested lead.

Space Ads:

Space ads are relatively expensive and should be used with caution and lots of testing to get them to work properly. If you can crack the code, you could have a real winner of a lead generation tool on your hands.

Most cities, regardless of size, have at least one weekly newspaper dedicated to business affairs. Many have trade journals locally based as well. Both options could be viable. Remember, the purpose of your ad is to generate a lead, not necessarily acquire a new member. Although that is the ultimate goal of each of your lead generation strategies, your immediate goal is to build a relationship with prospects by providing them with valuable information about the benefits of attending a group such as yours.

Attending Networking Meetings and Community Events:

Depending on the event, networking meetings can be a great way to meet new people looking for ways to build their own businesses and establish new relationships. The most likely impetus for generating leads at a networking event is collecting or giving out your own business cards.

If at all possible, I recommend collecting as many cards as you can because once you get back to your office you are going to transfer the information on those cards to your CRM database. Then you'll send out e-mails or letters, offering additional information and an invitation to a Mastermind meeting. This is where most people fail at these events. They get a handful of cards and then stuff them in a drawer when they get to the office, never doing anything with them. You have to be more strategic than that. Keep those cards and put together a plan to reach out and further the relationship.

Speaking Engagements:

Networking groups, business conferences, trade shows, and other event promoters are always looking for relevant, interesting speakers to provide valuable content to their attendees. This is one of the easiest and fastest ways to establish credibility, trust, and authority.

Finding these gigs is fairly easy, too. Since these organizers advertise in a lot of the same places you will, it's just a matter of sending them a letter or two explaining that you are an expert on the power of Mastermind Groups and have an interesting take on why everyone should leverage their own group. Put together a packet of info to send them, and offer to speak for free. You'll be surprised at how readily you are given the opportunity to speak to a group of perfect prospects. The best part is that someone else spent all of the time and money getting them in the same room together for you.

Along these same lines, you can also organize your own events where you can be the keynote speaker. I will show you how to do this as an additional revenue source, but it could also be used as a pure, lead generation tool.

Organize and host an event around a certain topic, make it free, and promote it through all of the same channels we're talking about here. You'll spend a little money doing this, but just view that as a marketing expense. Plus, you can line up sponsors to cover the costs. Events are great ways to leverage your time and get in front of a large group of potential prospects, all in one day.

Publicity:

Event promoters are always looking for speakers to present solid information to their groups. The same goes for news agencies. They have to fill up a news program or newspaper *every single day,* and believe me, they are begging for compelling content.

I have used publicity very successfully in the past, not just as a lead generation tool but also as a way to build credibility and authority. The logical assumption about people who are interviewed on a specific topic in the news is that they are experts. Otherwise, why would the news agency use them? This establishes instant trust among those who read and hear your opinions.

Another nice benefit of being featured in the news is that you now have content you can use in your own marketing. Whether it's an article, a video, or whatever, you can include it with your marketing materials, now adding an extra layer of trust, credibility, and authority.

You can also use publicity through community service-type events. These are free events you put on for community members who are not necessarily potential prospects for your Mastermind Group. The idea behind this strategy is to offer a valuable resource to those who may need it, while building your own image and goodwill in the community.

I'll give you two examples of workshops. The first is called "The Young Entrepreneur's Workshop." It is designed specifically for kids ages eleven to seventeen who are interested in starting their own business. The workshop runs for two days. The first day is filled with useful presentations on the mechanics of starting and running a small business. The second day is usually a field trip to a local business so the kids can get a behind-the-scenes look at how a small business is operated.

The second event is called "The Self-Reliance Initiative" and is for adults who are down on their luck, maybe on government assistance, or are otherwise struggling. This workshop is held once per week for four weeks and teaches the skills needed to become more self-reliant.

Neither event is geared towards likely Mastermind Group members, but in both cases I have been interviewed by the news media about the two workshops. This built a lot of goodwill and name recognition in my community. I still get recognized today by people who saw those segments on TV and who want to know more about them and about me. While I can't exactly point to a Mastermind member and say, "Yeah, he came to me from seeing me on TV," I have no doubt that the workshops have been beneficial to my business and will continue to be beneficial in the future.

Centers of Influence:

Centers of influence are influential members of your community who may not be a good fit with your Mastermind Groups, but have a lot of influence within a large pool of potential prospects and can recommend you to those people.

These could be upper-level managers of big companies who also happen to sit on the board of the local Rotary club, or they are politicians or board members of nonprofits that you are involved with. The point is, you probably know a group of these leaders already, so you'll need to go to work on building a solid relationship and serve them in whatever way you can.

This is just the tip of the iceberg when it comes to finding potential group members, but if you will put these eight into place, backed with a solid strategy for each one, you will have no trouble finding more Mastermind Group members than you know what to do with.

Now that you have found them, you need to give these potential members a compelling reason to find out more about your Mastermind meetings.

ATTRACT THEM

The days of simple transactional relationships, if they ever really existed, are long gone. Our economy has shifted so much over the last several years as to render this business model completely obsolete. Consumers nowadays are much more discerning and particular about where they will spend their money. It's not necessarily that they are cutting back on spending, but the hurdles business owners face now as opposed to even just four years ago are much more imposing and difficult to overcome.

The resistance of today's consumer demands a more sophisticated approach to marketing and selling, an approach that has an inviolable trust as the foundation. The only way to build trust is with value and time, and you are going to learn how to build that kind of trust with your prospects and attract them.

I use the word "attraction" very deliberately. In this business, the attraction of prospects is mandatory. If you cold call them, chase them, or try to manipulate them with slick sales copy or closing techniques, you are going to lose them forever. You must very intentionally build a relationship if you have any hope of gaining a group member.

Lead Generation "Magnets":

In order to attract qualified prospects, you are going to need tools to attract them. The easiest way to do this is by presenting information that is relevant and useful to your potential members. The Mastermind Group business is one predicated on a high level of trust.

You will begin building that trust first by being a provider of value, without necessarily expecting a sale to take place immediately. By doing this you are demonstrating expertise, authority, and the willingness to establish a trust-based relationship. Think of the value as magnets.

What do these lead generation magnets look like? They can be in virtually any format: reports, CDs, DVDs, booklets, webinars, or teleseminars. They just need to be highly informative, useful, and relatable to the subject of Masterminds.

You might create a free report entitled "Seven Ways to Grow Your Business through Strategic Partnerships" and detail that out for your potential members. One of the seven should be about Mastermind Groups, gently nudging the reader to learn more by requesting additional information from you. Your goal is to deliver high-quality information, but don't forget that you are also trying to sell them on taking action.

These reports or informational products can be distributed through the channels I listed in the previous section. After prospects have read your report, listened to an audio CD, or watched a DVD you have put together, their curiosity has been piqued and they will likely contact you to learn more. This is where you send them something a little more substantial.

The Shock 'n Awe Package:

Earlier I kept hinting about the time we would talk about exactly what to give interested prospects. I called it the "packet of information." This is it—the "Shock 'n Awe" package.

As you might have guessed, it is designed to do just what its name implies. Recipients should be wowed by the unique, valuable information you have provided for them, and by the fact that you went to such lengths to grab their attention. That's really what we're aiming at here . . . grabbing attention.

In the 1970s, it was estimated that we were subjected to around 1,000 ads per day. Today that number is closer to 5,000. We are constantly and unbelievably bombarded with ads all day long. It is absolutely critical that you stand out from the crowd and show up like no one else would dare.

What goes into this package of information? There is a valuable report that explains the concept of the Mastermind and benefits of being a member. This really sells them on the idea of belonging to a group. The report covers many of the same points I outlined in chapter 1 and goes inside a nice folder that is branded with my logo. Also inside the folder is a welcome letter explaining the contents of the packet.

Then I put in a copy of Napoleon Hill's book, *Think and Grow Rich*. It also has a bookmark inserted in where the chapter on Masterminds is. That bookmark has my contact info on it along with an inspirational quote.

Next, I found these decorative light bulbs with a flat bottom and a socket that unscrews from the bulb. These aren't real light bulbs; they are supposed to be used for decoration only. I also found a five-pound bag of real shredded money on the Internet. I unscrewed the socket part and stuffed the light bulb full of this shredded money, then screwed the socket back on. I attached a note to the bulb, explaining that the main purpose of a Mastermind Group is to take our ideas and turn them into money. I then encourage them to place the light bulb full of money on their desk or somewhere in their office so that they can see it every day and be reminded of the idea that as an entrepreneur, it is their nature to turn ideas into money.

A jump drive (USB drive) is included with my logo on it. On that jump drive, I load a short video of me thanking them for ordering our information, covering a few of the benefits of being in a Mastermind, and then include several video testimonials from some of my own Mastermind Group members.

The last thing I include—and this is very important—is a personal invitation to the next Mastermind meeting. Generally I will let first-time guests attend for free to see if the group is a good fit for them and to see if the other group members feel this new person will be a good fit for the group. This invitation will serve as your "call to action," an important step in converting an interested prospect into a paying group member.

Everything is put into a box with shredded packing paper to keep it in place and secure. My logo is on top of the box, along with the words "The Power of Mastermind Groups."

If this seems like a lot of effort and work, it is. That is intentional. You have a lot of work to do to cut through the clutter of the literally thousands of other marketing and advertising messages your prospects are subjected to on a daily basis. Our information kit stands out from the crowd and gets noticed.

Apart from that, it does a lot of the heavy lifting for me. That one package contains basically everything they need to learn all about Mastermind Groups and make a decision on whether or not to join. Once they have gone through the package, they are 90 percent sold. When I follow up with them a few days later, I don't have to "sell" them. I just answer questions and address any concerns they might have.

You have identified potential members, found them, and attracted interested prospects. Now it is time to convert them into paying group members.

CONVERT THEM

Every lead generated will come to you at a different point in the potential member's decision-making stage. We all have our own unique process for buying goods or services, and the resulting time frame is different for everyone. Some people make decisions fairly quickly with a limited amount of information. Others take months to decide, carefully and painstakingly piecing together as much information as they can before actually pulling the trigger on a purchase.

Your conversion process has to take this into account and address this from the very beginning, done through the Holy Grail of marketing: the art and science of follow-up.

Follow-up is one of the most important things you can do, yet is one of the least consistently utilized tools of most business owners. The key to follow-up is to be diligent without being obnoxious and aggressive without being too pushy. There is a delicate balance that needs to be observed that can only be established over time, after having experimented with different procedures through trial and error.

There are three main things you need to keep in mind to implement a successful business follow-up system:

1. You may tend to vastly underestimate how often and for how long your prospects will tolerate follow-up efforts. Many times you are so afraid of annoying them that you do far less follow-up than you should. Don't overdo it, but be a little more aggressive than what your gut tells you.

2. Use a variety of media to connect with prospects. When you offered your free information and Shock 'n Awe package, you should have collected as much info from your prospect as possible. Incorporate e-mail, phone calls, mailers, postcards, faxes, voice mail, and any other media you can into your follow-up plan.

3. Follow-up should be divided into two basic categories: short-term conversion efforts and long-term lead nurture. Every lead that comes through your office should be aggressively pursued and converted. You are not going to close every lead, so those that are not closed during your short-term, follow-up campaign should then be put on a longer-term drip campaign. In the short term, your lead may receive messages from you as frequently as every day to once a week for a three to six month period. After that, you will put them on a less frequent follow-up plan where you may only contact them twelve to fifteen times per year.

Effective marketing is going to either make or break your Mastermind Group business. Members will come and members will go, so you will always need to keep your pipeline full of potential prospects.

Keep in mind that your marketing plan needs to account for the four main functions: *identify potential members, find them, attract them,* and *convert them.* If you stick to this process, you should have no trouble keeping a waiting list of eager prospects ready to join your Mastermind Group.

In the next chapter, I will show you ways to leverage your original group and how to find access to additional revenue sources and profit centers to grow your business or to earn additional income.

CHAPTER 5:

USING YOUR MASTERMIND GROUP TO LEVERAGE ADDITIONAL REVENUE OPPORTUNITIES

When you picked up this book, you may have only done so because you run your own business and were looking for a little help getting a group together. This may have been for your own benefit or for the benefit of some friends. That is perfectly fine. If you never make a penny from your group members but continue to reap the benefits from being in a dynamic setting like this, it is all worth it.

Making money from a Mastermind Group may not have even been on your radar. But generating some additional income with Mastermind Groups is fairly easy to do, once you have your group assembled. You can implement several of the following revenue generation strategies at no cost to you, and that will take up very little of your time. Don't worry about implementing all of them. Pick those that appeal most and get started generating a little extra cash each month. If you are feeling ambitious, implement them all and add a few extra thousand dollars to your own income each and every month. It is up to you.

CONSULTING/STRATEGY DEVELOPMENT

Mastermind Groups are great for business and development strategies, but sometimes your group members will realize they need more one-on-one help on an ongoing basis. This is where you can offer weekly consulting services.

For my own clients, I do one-hour weekly consulting sessions, dedicated to nailing down their business strategy. We create to-do lists for completing each of the various components. My clients enjoy this arrangement because each week we are systematically working on their business, constructing very concrete steps to follow during the week. With my help, they form a plan, and then get their to-do list done that week.

I have found that although my Mastermind members are all very high-level thinkers, it really helps for things to be spelled out. Not because they can't do it themselves, but because they have so much on their plate already. If you can take the guesswork out of the equation, they will pay you handsomely for doing so. You can expect to charge anywhere from $100 to $250 an hour for your consulting services, depending on how much value your client feels you bring to the table.

Sometimes however, you will find that even though you are developing solid strategies and creating task lists for your clients, they still can't find the time or dedicate the resources (read: *employees*) toward getting them implemented. Doing it for them creates another great opportunity to generate additional revenue.

IMPLEMENTATION SERVICES

Entrepreneurs as a group are a funny bunch. It seems that most of the ones I know—including me—are great starters but have a hard time finishing projects or tasks. A lot of us suffer from what I call "shiny object syndrome," which makes us jump from project to project every time something newer and more exciting comes along.

Simply put, a lot of us have problems actually implementing the various ideas we get from the Mastermind Group. Don't get me wrong; we still implement a whole lot more than most people do. If we could somehow implement at a much higher level, our businesses would grow exponentially.

One of the first things you can provide would be turnkey, "done-for-you" type services. Since most of your Mastermind Group members will be actively trying to grow their businesses, the most logical area to start with is their marketing campaigns.

There are so many little details to be taken care of when implementing a full-blown marketing plan. The task can seem overwhelming. There's an old adage in the marketing world that says, "If you give a consumer too many choices to make, he ends up not making any choice at all." This applies to big projects as well. If there are too many tasks in a project, you may feel overwhelmed by the complexity and enormity of it all, and take no action at all. You may very well eat an elephant by taking one bite at a time, but seeing that great, hulking mass of grey flesh sitting in front of you can be daunting. It is much more easily said than done.

The fact of the matter is that most business owners are begging for someone to help them get their marketing implemented and firing on all cylinders.

Any of those little details that you can get done for a business owner is a chance to not only help that business out, but for you to generate additional revenue. The task list is virtually endless and hard to do it all unless you own an actual marketing company. Here are some that you can do without the need for any special equipment.

COPYWRITING

Writing sales copy is a must-have skill for any business owner, but most owners do not study this discipline much. If you are skilled at writing sales copy, you can write all the different components of your members' marketing plans. This might include copy for sales letters, postcards, landing pages, websites, brochures, and booklets. Even if business owners do know how to write copy, it can be tedious, and they are often relieved to hand the chore off to someone else.

DIRECT MAIL

You may not own a print shop, but a lot of work goes into getting direct mail pieces put together and out the door. Besides copywriting—the actual writing of the piece— someone needs to fold letters, stuff envelopes, stamp them, and deliver them to the post office. In some cases, you may even need to sort and bundle them before delivering them to be mailed. This manual labor may not be something business owners want to do themselves and may not even want their staff to do. So, you get it done for them.

SOCIAL MEDIA MANAGEMENT

Managing social media can be a huge time-suck for business owners, because they don't usually see any immediate, direct benefit from using Facebook, Twitter, LinkedIn, or any of the other hundreds of social media sites. But it certainly can be useful to businesses that do it right and *do it consistently*. Again, this is an area they will willingly outsource, so neither they nor their employees have to spend time on it.

BLOGGING

The next wave in business is not necessarily new. In fact, the most successful small businesses have been doing this for a while now, and that is creating and publishing useful content to be consumed by their prospects and customers. Blogging is a great media for getting out fresh, new content on a regular basis. It is similar to social media in that most business owners don't see any immediate return on their investment, so it is something easy to push down the priority list. Outsourcing it to you is a great way for business owners to make sure the blogging is done on a consistent and regular basis.

MONTHLY NEWSLETTERS (ENEWSLETTERS OR HARD COPY NEWSLETTERS)

Newsletters are one of the best, yet least utilized, marketing tools available to a small business. Although I prefer and recommend that my clients use a hard copy of monthly newsletters, you can also create and send electronic newsletters via e-mail. Finding content and writing newsletters for your group members are great ways to help them maintain regular contact with their customers and select prospects.

PUBLICITY AND PUBLIC RELATIONS

Any business on the planet can benefit from publicity and public relations. Unfortunately, a lot of business owners don't feel like they can get their company recognized by the media. But they can, and it's much easier than you think. As I said before, media outlets are desperate for good, solid content to present to their viewers, listeners, or readers. The area where you can really help a group member is not only in creating or writing the press release, but also in coming up with a newsworthy angle the media will want to cover.

Approach it like a reporter and see if you can find a compelling story lurking somewhere in your member's business. Then put it down on paper and get it into the hands of your local news agencies.

EVENT PLANNING

Grand openings of new stores, customer appreciation events, and other events are an excellent way for you to generate additional revenue. Many times your Mastermind Group members have never done an event before and have no idea even where to begin. You can help them plan and execute their event so they need only concentrate on being there and being with their customers or prospects.

You can handle virtually everything from creating the invitations to hiring the caterer to securing the venue. It takes a lot of work to host a successful event, so your services in this area will be welcomed.

There are obviously many other areas where you can pitch in and help out, but what if you don't have the equipment or

Affiliate arrangements

expertise to implement them for your group member? That's where affiliate arrangements come into play.

AFFILIATE ARRANGEMENTS

An affiliate arrangement is simply a business arrangement that allows you to earn a commission on any business you have generated for your affiliate partner. For example, if you have a group member putting together a direct mail campaign, you may contract with a local print shop to do the printing. Your commission may be anywhere from 10 to 20 percent for something like this.

You can outsource virtually anything: graphic design, printing, copywriting, web design, telemarketing, social media management, e-mail database management, autoresponder software, programming services, promotional items, search engine optimization, and pay-per-click management. Any one of these—and many others—can be contracted out to freelancers or companies specializing in each of these areas. Most will be willing to set up an affiliate arrangement with you. It's as simple as asking them about it.

You can also earn commissions on any advertising expenditures that your client has. This includes advertising on television, radio, in magazines, trades journals, and newspapers. Each of these types of media work with advertising agencies and even have a 15 percent commission built into their pricing. So if you have a client spending $3,000 a month to run radio ads, you will automatically get $450 of that every single month. That's pretty easy money.

You may be wondering why a client would have you do these services if you are just going to outsource them to others. The answer is simple: it is just more work for them to do, and they would rather have you manage the various components instead of doing it themselves. If you build a dynamic network of different companies to implement these various tasks, then clients will pay you to access that network. It's easier to pay you than trying to piecemeal different providers together and manage everything on top of that.

Keep in mind that your reputation is on the line when you recommend any company for outsourcing. Use only reputable companies that are established and have great customer reviews and those companies you have used yourself or have been referred to you by people you trust.

PRIVATE COACHING

Private coaching is very similar to traditional business consulting or strategy development. The main difference is the latter focuses on business growth and systems, where private coaching focuses on the entrepreneur himself. Coaching has more to do with mindset, personal growth, and designing a life outside of the business. It has to do with creating a purposeful life of finding happiness and maintaining balance in the face of the many demands of life.

Many business owners do not give these areas the time and attention they deserve, but they are crucial to living a meaningful life. Sometimes it just helps to talk these things out and bounce ideas off one another.

Other times you need to be more structured. Two tools that I use often are Vision Boards and Mind Maps. They both serve essentially the same purpose but are slightly different in format. You start with a basic idea, concept, or thing, and that becomes the center of focus. If you are working on yourself, then the object of focus is going to be you. From there, you work on all of the different areas of your life. These could be things like mindset, character, and habits but will also include things like family, friends, and goals. The idea here is to design your life, in visual form, and then strategize all the ways you can accomplish those things or develop the behaviors you need to make that vision come true. This is a powerful way to get more focused and hold yourself accountable for your own growth.

The perfect coaching client is one who practices what is called the "slight-edge" principle. Whenever I mention coaching as a revenue source, one of the most common objections is why would an already successful entrepreneur hire someone to coach them on becoming successful? I tell them it is because of this slight-edge principle.

Successful people are successful because they are always looking for new ways, tools, and resources for becoming more successful. They understand that success is an ongoing process, not a one-time event. They also know that the moment they feel as if they have "arrived," they are sure to start losing ground and regressing. Because of this, they are always looking for that next big thing to give them a slight edge in business and life. Your coaching program can scratch that perpetual itch they have to always be better.

Coaching sessions can be held weekly, but are more often done two to three times per month. As with consulting, you can expect to charge $100 to $150 an hour.

SPECIALTY WORKSHOPS

In chapter 3, I gave you a series of topics to talk about in your Mastermind Groups. However, you will typically only spend around thirty to forty-five minutes on those presentations. While you can give a good, solid overview of the material, you aren't going to be able to dig in deep and really explore it in depth.

You may want to use specialty workshops centered on certain topics that run for two to three hours. This allows you to dedicate a good chunk of time to topics that your members find relevant. The workshops also allow you to charge an additional fee for putting them on, anywhere from $49 up to $199, depending on how valuable and in-demand the information is.

Here are several workshop ideas you may consider.

LEAD GENERATION STRATEGIES

The absolute, number one thing small business owners say they need help with most is new lead generation or customer acquisition ideas and strategies. Most small business owners are very sporadic and nonstrategic when it comes to generating leads or acquiring new customers, so this type of workshop will always be in demand.

SOCIAL MEDIA MARKETING

I include this topic because it just happens to be the hottest thing on the business landscape right now. By the time you read this, it could very well be something else, and I recommend you go with that new shiny object, whatever it may be.

That being said, I don't believe social media is going anywhere anytime soon. I believe its uses will evolve over time, but it will probably continue to be part of a business's marketing mix, so it is worthy of our attention.

SEARCH ENGINE OPTIMIZATION

If you want to look like a hero relatively quickly, then teach your Mastermind Group members how to get their websites ranked in the top five of the major search engines like Google, Bing, and Yahoo. Most local businesses do this very poorly, and getting ranked in the top five for local search terms is a relatively easy task. It can also be a massive traffic generator and lead generation machine if used properly.

CONTENT CREATION

Small businesses that are going to win now and in the future are those that become quasi-publishing companies. They must be willing—and able—to churn out relevant, useful content on an ongoing basis. Teaching business owners how to create free reports, audio, video, blogs, and other content will be extremely important to their long-term success.

FINANCIAL PLANNING STRATEGIES

These workshops don't necessarily have to be all about marketing strategies, however. Many business owners need help with financial planning for both themselves and their business. A workshop or series of workshops covering financial planning, insurance needs, tax mitigation strategies, and others will be of very high value to entrepreneurs who want to learn the best way to keep and grow their hard-earned money.

HIRING/FIRING/TRAINING EMPLOYEES

Dealing with employees can be a huge source of frustration for business owners, and most of us are poorly equipped to handle the myriad of problems associated with maintaining a staff. Most business schools don't really address how to handle employees either, so we are basically left to our own devices and intuition. Employees can make or break a company, especially a small company, so acquiring the skills to deal with them effectively is very valuable indeed.

TIME MANAGEMENT

Everyone—I don't care who you are—can get better about managing his or her time. Time is the one great equalizer. I may not have the money or resources that a Bill Gates or a Warren Buffett has, but we all have the same exact hours in our day. The biggest difference between the super successful and the mediocre majority is how the two groups manage their time. Well-managed time leads to higher productivity, bigger profits, and greater business growth.

Having a well-run Mastermind Group with dedicated members can be great for your business and self-growth and can be a lot of fun, but it also offers a diverse range of ways to generate additional profits. These profits can become big enough to create another business entirely or modest enough to just give you some extra cash in your pocket each month. The choice is yours.

In the next chapter we'll talk about taking your Mastermind Group to the next level with retreats, boot camps, events, and specific niches.

CHAPTER 6:

ADVANCED MASTERMIND GROUP PRINCIPLES: TAKING IT TO THE NEXT LEVEL

One of the main themes discussed in this book is growing yourself and your company through the power of the Mastermind. I don't mean physically, as in grow your company size, although that may very well be something you strive for. What I mean is to grow in the metaphysical sense, such as growing beyond where you are today . . . in mindset, in spirit, in service, in wealth, and in happiness.

My philosophy on life is that you have to keep growing or you die. It's that simple.

I believe most people go through life striving to reach one goal after another. When they stop striving, their body and mind give up and they literally die.

Running a Mastermind Group gives you a vehicle for stretching yourself, your mind, and your business in ways you could not alone. In this chapter, I will talk about some additional means for taking your group to the next level, and then the next, and the next, and so on.

You can view these options as just that, options. Feel free to add as many or few as you'd like. Change them, modify them, add to them, take away from them—use this as a guide to create a way for you to best expand your own thinking and cater to your particular needs and goals.

I'm going to give you four different ideas in this chapter: retreats, boot camps, events, and niche Mastermind Groups. Each will offer its own unique benefits and help meet the particular goals you may have. My advice is to implement them one at a time so as not to stretch your time and resources too thin and to get them up and running smoothly one by one. Once you have your system down, add another one and so on.

RETREATS

In college, I read Henry David Thoreau's collection of essays in the book *Walden* and was moved by his take on life. He urged us to simplify, simplify, simplify. Over the years I got caught up in the proverbial rat race and quest for more. More money, more business, more house, more everything. I lost sight of the fact that those things, in and of themselves, wouldn't make me happy. I chased them anyway.

Over time I occasionally returned to Thoreau's words and reset my life, my mind, and my soul. I found it helpful to get away for a few days, either alone or with my family, and used that time to get out of the hustle and bustle of the everyday, turning an introspective eye on my life. I used that time to get clear about whom I was and whom I still wanted to be, and to define my life's true purpose.

Although I didn't label these excursions as such at the time, what I was really creating was a retreat: a retreat from life and the pressures, stressors, and problems that go along with a busy and occupied existence.

I firmly believe that if you are not clear and focused in all aspects of your life, your business will suffer as a result. Retreats are a great way to get away from everything and take time to focus on the little external influences outside of your business. Things like health, relationships, wealth, family, exercise, mindset, and spirituality.

I have the good fortune of living in Boise, Idaho. About an hour or so north of here is a little town called McCall. It's a beautiful place nestled next to a large lake and somewhat in the mountains. I love heading to our cabin up there and being away from the bigger city of Boise. McCall is just far enough away to be removed from it all and small enough to really be able to get inside yourself and reflect.

For your Mastermind Group members, a fun way to make this happen is to rent a large cabin (or two if coed: one for the men and one for the women) and make the trip together. You can hire a caterer in town to prepare your meals for you or go shopping and plan a menu to cook. The food at these retreats is very important. Not only are you going to want to make delicious yet healthy meals, you are also going to need to be aware of any allergies, food, or other health issues that could cause attendees problems.

The next thing to consider is your agenda during the time you will be there. I recommend that you make your retreat at least three days and two nights long. This will give you a good chunk of time to get some excellent work done, but will be short enough for anyone wanting to get away who is hesitant about being gone for too long.

As far as content goes, this is fairly simple. You are essentially going to expand on the topics covered in your Mastermind meetings. Let's say that during one of your Mastermind meetings, you explored the topic of "The Power of Positive Thinking." That presentation might have lasted only thirty to forty-five minutes. Now you could easily dedicate two to three hours to it. You could also incorporate a group exercise or other appropriate activity.

Remember, you will have an entire day or more, so you will need at least two to three presentations and other activities to fill in the time. Don't forget to schedule break times and time for meals and socializing. Keep a brisk, yet relaxed, pace going throughout the day. Have practical and useful sessions, but also allow time for fun activities. For example, in McCall we might schedule an entire morning or afternoon to go skiing or something similar. At night we might all head over to a local watering hole and have some time for drinks and conversation.

Spend time on the mind–body connection. Incorporate some time for meditation, yoga, massage, or other activities along these lines that might appeal to your group members.

Your goal with a retreat such as this is to completely "wow" them and make their time with you as memorable as possible. This means that you have to do everything in your power to make it a killer experience. When they leave to go back home, not only should they feel rejuvenated and clear about their future, they should also be so excited about their experience that they feel compelled to tell others.

The price charged for your retreats will vary depending on the level and types of services you incorporate. Buying food and cooking it yourself probably won't cost as much as hiring a caterer or chef to cook for you, but it will take more time. You will have to decide exactly how much work you want to do or have time to do. Taking that into consideration, you will probably want to charge anywhere from $500 to $2,000 total per person.

BOOT CAMPS

Where retreats are more about mindset, mind–body connection, improving yourself, and other such topics, boot camps are more about practical, relevant, and useful skill acquisition.

Boot camp topics are usually very specific and focused on one realm of business or marketing. It could be a boot camp that teaches lead generation strategies, how to use Google AdWords, how to use landing pages to capture e-mail addresses, or how to make money with Facebook ads. It could be how to hire, train, and retain key employees. Or it might be about tax strategies specifically for small businesses of a certain size. After you have been running your Mastermind Groups for a while, you will get a pretty good idea which topics are most appealing to spend additional time developing.

Like retreats, boot camps will last anywhere from two to four days and will typically run from 8 a.m. or 9 a.m. until 4 p.m. or 5 p.m. Lunch is typically served along with plenty of snacks and beverages throughout the day.

During your boot camp, you will probably want to enlist the help of outside speakers or presenters. Apart from being physically exhausting for you if you do all the presenting, group members will appreciate hearing from other speakers. Incorporate several individual and/or group sessions where you give attendees time to work on the things you have discussed. You could include checklists, worksheets, how-to templates, and other similar collateral material.

For the venue, just about any location will work. Hotel conference rooms are the most obvious selection since they are usually conveniently located, have a wide array of available services (projectors, Internet hookup, etc.), and will be able to provide catering for lunch and any other meals.

The price point for boot camps will also vary, just as they do with retreats, but you can plan on charging around $300 to $1,000 or more. Some big-name gurus command up to $5,000 for a three-day boot camp, but don't expect anything like that right out of the gate. The exception would be if you are bringing in a famous speaker to justify that type of price, but those are few and far between. For now, stick with the lower price range and make sure you not only cover your costs but also build in a decent margin for yourself.

OTHER EVENTS

Other events can be very similar to boot camps or retreats but are typically much shorter in duration and intensity. For example, you may decide to hold an event geared towards helping business owners generate leads online. This event may be held during the evening from 6 p.m. to 8 p.m., or something along those lines. These can either be one-off events (special events that are only held one time) or a series of events held over a certain period of time (i.e., four to six weeks).

As with boot camps and retreats, you will want to consider meal options (or at least snacks and drinks), an appropriate venue, materials that need to be created (worksheets, checklists, manuals, etc.), and any guest speakers you would like to invite. Along the line of speakers, you may have Mastermind members who are experts in a particular field help you with presenting content. This gives you informative, useful content and your speakers a way to hone their presentation skills.

A spin-off of that idea is to actually create an event that you cohost with one or more of your Mastermind members. For example, I once cohosted an event with two of my Mastermind Group members, one a financial advisor and the other a CPA. The event was presented to business owners to teach them about marketing, business planning, and tax issues for small businesses. We used the event as a lead generation tool for each of our businesses and split the cost of the event between the three of us.

You can really get creative with ideas for these events. You may decide to do a breakfast get-together that runs from 6 a.m. to 8 a.m., or take a field trip to visit a local business for a behind-the-scenes look at their operations. It is important to remember your events should not only be filled with useful and informative content, but should also be fun and entertaining.

Business events are a dime a dozen nowadays and frankly, most of them are pretty dry and boring.

Step outside of your comfort zone a little and create some excitement and fun for your group members or prospects.

Pricing for the event will obviously vary, depending on your audience and what kind of content is being presented. It is pretty standard to charge $49 to $99 for a one-time event, although you could probably get away with charging up to $300 or more for a series of events based on one topic.

If using the event as a lead generation tool, you might want to either make it free or charge something nominal. There are two schools of thought here: First, if you make it free you will get more people to attend, but they may not be the most ideal client for you. Second, by charging a nominal amount, you will discourage potential attendees, but that may be okay since it qualifies those who pay as being serious. Test both ways and see which one works the best for what you are trying to accomplish.

Two more ideas to consider...

These ideas don't really fit with those already covered in this chapter, but both are great ways to take your Mastermind Groups to the next level. They are niche Mastermind Groups and virtual Mastermind Groups.

NICHE MASTERMIND GROUPS

In the marketing chapter, you learned about narrowing your focus down to business owners who met certain criteria. You'll recall that the best candidates are ones who are into self-improvement, who are aggressive marketers, and who are somewhat established in business.

A fourth criterion to consider is more demographic in nature. Demographics are simply the objective, identifiable traits of a business or individual. Age, income, marital status, race/ethnicity, homeowner, or renter, are all demographics of individuals. Revenue, employee size, asset size, and industry type are all demographics of businesses. What does this have to do with your Mastermind Group?

Well, one thing I have learned in marketing is that the more you can tailor your product or service to a particular group, the better. Your marketing needs to speak directly to that person so that they feel like, "Hey, that product/service is for *me!*"

You can do this by creating Mastermind Groups around certain demographic characteristics. For example, you could form a group that is only for Hispanic business owners or for women business owners.

You may decide to form a group for businesses that target certain kinds of consumers. I'm thinking of a group that maybe only sells luxury, high-end goods that targets affluent, older clientele. Members of this group could be a jeweler, a yacht dealer, a financial advisor, and a luxury car dealership . . . you get the point.

You could form a group reserved for service professionals: attorneys, CPAs, or financial planners. Or a group of medical professionals like dentists, doctors, or chiropractors.

There are lots of little niche groups like this that you could form, each with their own unique reason for being, but all united by some common bond apart from being business owners. When you start speaking directly to these business owners and tailoring your groups specifically to them, you will find it much easier to form multiple groups in all of these different niches.

The nice thing about creating niche Mastermind Groups is that they are not only easier to sell, they also have greater price elasticity. The idea of "This is exactly for me!" gives you much greater flexibility in your pricing; that is, you can usually charge more. On an intuitive level this makes sense. A book titled *How to Make Money Investing in Real Estate* will sell for one price, but a book titled *How to Make Money Investing in Real Estate for Doctors* can be sold at a higher price, sometimes much higher.

Experiment a little with your niche group pricing to see if you can charge more for them. I think you will be surprised to find that you can charge more with absolutely no push-back from prospects.

VIRTUAL MASTERMIND GROUPS

You may feel you are in a market that is only so big and won't support more than one or two Mastermind Groups. Maybe you live in a small town or rural area. In that case, you can create long-distance groups done through group conference calls or even over the Internet.

One way I use this virtual Mastermind Group concept is with what I call "Accountability Calls." These calls usually have anywhere from three to five people on them and last approximately an hour and a half and are conducted once per month.

Each person on the call has three or four goals they wanted to accomplish during the previous month. They spend the first half of their allotted time talking about the goals and tasks they have completed, things they still need to finish, and any changes to the tasks they set during the previous month. They also bring up any challenges, problems, or opportunities that arose during the month relating to those goals or tasks and get input from the group for ideas on how best to address them. The second part of their allotted time is spent creating new goals for the upcoming month and the associated tasks with each that need to be completed. Individual group members take turns until everyone has had a chance to speak.

This is a fantastic way for these business owners to meet in a friendly environment and to hold themselves and other group members accountable each month. I do these meetings over the phone, but you could just as easily hold them online in a chat forum or some other similar online venue.

You could charge anywhere from $49 to $99 for this service, depending on how many members you have on each call or Internet chat. The nice thing about a setup like this is that you can do it from anywhere in the world you happen to be and can pull group members from a wide variety of industries, backgrounds, and even different countries.

The whole intent of forming a Mastermind Group is to stretch yourself and your business to new heights, whatever that means to you and your group members. You should constantly be on the lookout for ways to bring exciting new ideas and content to your group members in a variety of formats, whether that is through retreats, boot camps, other events, or even through a distance program.

In the next chapter you are going to have the opportunity to hear from some actual Mastermind Group members who will tell you in their own words why they feel joining a Mastermind Group is so important. You'll also hear of the specific benefits they have received from being part of a Mastermind Group. Pay close attention to their answers, take note of what they have said, and apply that to your own marketing messages to recruit prospective group members.

CHAPTER 7:

CONVERSATIONS WITH MASTERMIND GROUP MEMBERS

When you begin your marketing push to attract new members to your Mastermind Group, you will need to be very in tune with the messages you are communicating. If you get the exact messaging right, you will stand a much higher chance of getting the attention of a potential group member. Being off on your messaging—even just a little—can derail your entire marketing plan.

I took some time to interview just a few of my own Mastermind Group members and asked them questions about how being a part of a Mastermind Group has helped their business. I think you will find their answers instructive when you begin crafting your own marketing messages.

Here are five common themes identified during the Q&A process:

1. Benefits of joining the group
2. Accountability
3. Mindset
4. Implementation of ideas
5. Cost/Time concerns

Let me first introduce the members so that you have a better idea of whom they are and what their business is all about.

ADAM FEIK—BEACON ROCK INVESTMENT CONSULTING

Adam is the founder of Beacon Rock Investment Consulting, a full-service financial advisory firm. Prior to starting Beacon Rock, Adam worked as a broker for Piper Jaffray and later Wachovia Securities.

When asked why he wanted to join a Mastermind Group, Adam said, "I just wanted to be in a room with other business owners who were interested in working on their business and not just in it. I thought they probably faced similar challenges or opportunities as I was and knew it would be good to surround myself with like-minded people. Just to be able to bounce ideas off one another. I really wasn't sure if it would be a good fit for me, so I figured I would at least give it a shot and try it out. I'm really glad I did."

To read more about Adam, visit www.BeaconRockLLC.com.

VICTORIA SAVAGE—CARE FOR LIVING

Victoria is known by her clients as "Nurse Savage" because of her fierce advocacy of the senior population. Being an RN for more than twenty years gave Victoria a very detailed glimpse into the problems and challenges facing seniors.

She created Care for Living to address those issues. Care for Living is a full-service geriatric care firm that provides in-home assistance to seniors who are unable to continue caring for themselves.

When asked about joining the Mastermind Group Victoria replied, "I'm a nurse, not a business woman or marketer. The whole process of how to market my business was very, very gray to me and joining the Mastermind Group seemed like the quickest way to advance that learning curve. I really just needed help focusing on that specific part of my business."

You can learn more about Victoria and Care for Living at www.Care-For-Living.com.

ANDREW WHEELER—ECOSPACE MARKETING

Andrew's company, EcoSpace Marketing, is centered on the niche of "green" businesses such as contractors, architects, roofers, and other like companies that place an emphasis on being environmentally friendly. Andrew focuses on helping them develop and implement a strong online marketing presence.

"I had been in Mastermind Groups before and knew their power," Andrew said when asked about why he joined our group. "I know how much you can leverage other people's knowledge, insights, and experience to create your own take on an idea and implement it in your business however you see fit."

More about Andrew and EcoSpace Marketing can be found at www.EcoSpaceMarketing.com.

As you can see, there are several core ideas on why these entrepreneurs decided to join the group in the first place—the ability to be around like-minded individuals who were facing similar circumstances, shortening the learning curve, and leveraging their ideas were just a few of the reasons they gave.

Now let's dig into the main categories listed above.

BENEFITS OF JOINING A MASTERMIND GROUP

In an earlier chapter, I listed specific benefits that come from joining a Mastermind Group. They included:

- The ability to work on your business instead of just in it

- Camaraderie and understanding

- Unique perspectives

- Motivation

- Accumulated experience

- Ability to serve

- Accountability

The members had their own unique take on how they have profited from the group.

I use the term "profited" very loosely, referring not just to a specific monetary gain. Benefits that all three members expressed in different ways were the focus and clarity they get from the monthly meetings. This is really just a by-product of taking time to think strategically (working on your business) as opposed to just tactically (working in your business).

As Victoria Savage put it, "Being in the Mastermind Group has really helped me put a solid game plan together; it's helped me see the bigger picture instead of getting caught up in the minute details of it all."

Adam from Beacon Rock had a slightly different take. "What I really like is the fact that I get to see what others are doing in their businesses," he said, "then I can easily adapt or tweak that to apply it to my company. This has really cut down on the time it takes to develop an idea and get it implemented."

Another benefit uncovered through the interviews was having a like-minded peer group to bounce ideas off of during meetings.

"Being part of the Mastermind Group is about getting work done, but it's actually a lot of fun too," said Andrew Wheeler of EcoSpace Marketing. "Being able to connect and network with other entrepreneurs who are experiencing similar challenges is comforting."

I think it is important to remember that although you are starting your Mastermind Group to help your members grow their businesses, it is crucial to know that you are also providing them a safe haven where they can connect with others who are in similar situations in life. Everyone wants to belong to and identify with a group where they feel understood and connected. A Mastermind Group is the perfect place to do that.

Famed copywriter Cavett Robert once said, "People are wandering around with their umbilical cord in their hand looking for a place to plug it in. You can make a lot of money being the person that gives them a place to plug into."

As you set about trying to attract members for your Mastermind Group, you would do well to remember Robert's words. Weave that feeling of belonging and being a part of something where they are understood throughout your marketing copy. Communicating that sense of belonging is key to making that deeper connection with prospective members.

ACCOUNTABILITY

Being an entrepreneur can afford you an enormous amount of freedom to do things your way. To work where and when you want. To be who you want to be. Simply to live life the way you see fit.

But as Peter Parker's uncle told him, "With great power comes great responsibility." You have no one looking over your shoulder, holding your feet to the fire, pushing you to get things done. For success to be yours, you have to be a very self-motivated individual. You have to hold yourself responsible for doing what needs to be done.

This is hard for a lot of us. There is no doubt that we could all be more efficient with our time and get more done each day. Let's face it. It's sometimes easy to slack when we don't have anyone who holds us accountable for our actions.

Mastermind Groups, however, are the perfect vehicle for providing that measure of accountability, which may be lacking in your business life. It's embarrassing to go to the Mastermind meeting and get several actionable ideas and then return to your business and not get any of them done.

"I feel that when you have the group support behind you and the other members helping you make plans for your business, it would be disrespectful to return the following month without having done anything," Victoria remarked.

I agree. Fortunately, as entrepreneurs, most of us are intensely prideful and competitive human beings. I, for one, would rather have my arm cut off than lose face in the group that way.

For some, that measure of accountability is the driving force behind arriving at the heights they have reached. In fact, Adam Feik saw it this way, "I used to just get these little thoughts or ideas pop into my head all the time. Before, I would rarely get them out and jot them down or talk about them, and I certainly never acted on them. But since joining the Mastermind Group and sharing those ideas and my plans with the others, it has forced me to start implementing them."

In your marketing efforts you will want to be sure to emphasize this benefit, but make it clear that members are held accountable in a friendly, positive, and encouraging way. We want to be held accountable, but not if it means being embarrassed or made to feel uncomfortable.

MINDSET

One of the most rewarding aspects of leading a Mastermind Group—apart from seeing the tangible results like increased sales and profitability—is just the way members' mindsets shift as they adopt the principles being taught.

You can almost see the light bulbs turning on at each meeting as a new and deeper understanding of how businesses operate is realized. This is exciting and creates a positive energy and enthusiasm for the whole group.

Adam put it best when he said, "My mindset has shifted in a number of different ways. Before, someone would call me and say, 'Oh you should advertise here or here' or whatever and I probably would have done it, just not knowing any better. But, now I can see clearly whether or not it fits my overall business strategy. I know exactly what kind of client will make a great Beacon Rock client and who will not. Then I direct my dollars towards attracting that type of client. I now have answers to what type of client that is, what I should say to him, where I will find him, and so on."

A key word in Adam's statement is "attracting." Many times in business, owners are very reactionary, meaning they simply react to events as they unfold before them. This oftentimes includes accepting any new customer, client, or patient that comes along. This is done without thinking through the long-term ramifications of whether or not they are a good fit for each other.

This is born directly from a mindset that says you have to settle for or accommodate any potential prospects that come your way. However, you are free to choose any type of client you want. The number one reason you do not is because of fear. You fear losing money, offending people, or going against your inherent nature to accept any client.

A Mastermind Group is a great place to break those chains and decide to do business on your own terms, with the support and encouragement of a group that thinks and feels as you do.

This shift in mindset is sometimes very difficult to attain alone. Having group members who understand what you are going through makes it that much easier.

Along those same lines, being a part of a group allows you to expand your thinking and start to see things differently. Case in point, Andrew said, "When I first came to the group, my business model was fairly complicated and convoluted. As the other members began asking me questions, it forced me to clarify and focus my efforts and ultimately trim down some of my offerings. My business is much more streamlined and nimble. I'm not being pulled in several different directions anymore and have been able to refocus on our core reason for existing."

Again, your mindset is established by what you see, hear, and learn in the world. Sometimes, what is expected of you clouds your vision, but being part of a group that helps you see things in a different way is immensely valuable.

IMPLEMENTATION OF IDEAS

In Robert Ringer's book, *Action: Nothing Happens until Something Moves*, he recounts a story he heard about Paul Simon of Simon and Garfunkel fame. Simon had just come out with a new record based on the tribal sounds of Africa. During an interview with a reporter, he was asked how he felt about the critics who said he had done nothing special, that he had simply done what anyone could have done, which was take existing African sounds and package them into an album.

Simon's response was, "Maybe it's true that anyone *could* have done it, but I *did* it."

Ideas, even great ideas, are a dime a dozen.
Without implementation—without action—those ideas
are ultimately worthless.

There's something about being part of an action-oriented group that lights a fire under you and gets you going. There are very few places where you can find this more consistently than in a Mastermind Group.

"I look at what we discuss and the different avenues available to us. We talk a lot about the [marketing] funnel and how to funnel all these into a revenue stream. I then take them step by step on a daily basis so that I can work to achieve the different ideas and the goals that we set in the group," said Victoria.

Business can be overwhelming and time-consuming. The only way to eat an elephant is one bite at a time. Victoria's method of implementing ideas she gets from the group on a daily, step-by-step basis is the best approach. It is easy to get overwhelmed and discouraged with the amount of work that needs to be done and not do it at all.

The game is won, however, by those willing to do the things that others can't or won't do. This is easier said than done but gets easier to do when you are part of a group that is cheering you along and holding you accountable.

I firmly believe you can almost always overcome lack of talent, lack of education, and lack of resources with good, old-fashioned elbow grease. If you look around at some of the more successful people you know in your life and analyze what sets them apart, I think you will find that in most cases, it is their ability to get things done.

Keep this in mind when recruiting members for your Mastermind Group. You want those individuals who have a great work ethic and will be master implementers. Their natural enthusiasm for work will spread to the other group members and everyone in turn will benefit.

COST AND TIME CONCERNS

The two biggest excuses I get when talking to potential Mastermind Group members are the costs involved and the time commitment. Invariably, these are going to be the two main objections you receive as well.

First, let's not kid ourselves. Being an entrepreneur is extremely time-consuming. It seems like there is no end to meetings, deadlines, and emergencies that crop up. Finding the time to work on your business seems like an uphill battle from the get-go.

Second, charging someone $300 to $1,000 a month to sit around and talk to other people may seem foolish to some.

We know however, that it is crucial to plan and strategize and it is helpful to get the support and feedback from a group, so I asked the members about their thoughts on the time and financial commitment they make each month to attend the meeting.

"You're going to have to work on your business in order to be successful anyway," Adam reasoned, "so it's going to be more costly if you make avoidable mistakes along the way. If you look at the numbers, *not* joining a Mastermind will probably be ultimately more costly in the long run than spending the money to join one will. To me, it makes much more sense to take the time and spend the money on a group and limit or avoid those costly mistakes in the first place."

Victoria put it in a different perspective, "The time commitment is only four hours per month. I mean, if you can't invest that in your business, then maybe you should rethink being in business because that is a minimal commitment for any business owner to put in to have an avenue to grow their business."

As a business owner, you often have a dual responsibility. You not only have to do the work required to make sales, deliver product, or serve customers, but you also have to develop and direct the strategy for moving your business forward. Employees don't have to worry about the second part of that equation.

Those skills aren't something you normally learn as part of a job or in school (even business school); you have to pick them up along the way. If you don't take the time to learn them, then your business will fail. It's really that simple.

To sum up, I think Andrew really put it well when he said,

> "The risk of not joining a Mastermind Group is you're going to end up spending the next five years going down a rabbit hole that you maybe could have avoided.

Someone five years ago could have directed you down a different trajectory, which would have put you on a whole different course today. From personal experience, I know that dredging it solo rarely works out because you don't have all the answers. The entrepreneurs who are successful borrow from other people, get advice from other people, and get help. That's really what you need, help with your business. If you're not as successful as you would like today, then you really should consider joining a Mastermind Group."

You have to keep in mind that you are helping real people solve real problems in their businesses. I hope hearing from actual Mastermind Group members who are in the trenches of their business every day has helped you see what a valuable service you are providing by starting a group of your own.

CHAPTER 8:

BEGIN YOUR JOURNEY TODAY

When I think back on my early business career, I look back at a kid who, although armed with a business degree, was wandering around pretty clueless about life in general and business in particular. I was a kid who had big dreams, grand hopes, and a burning desire to succeed, but it was a pretty lonely existence.

All of my friends left college to search for a "regular" job and just didn't understand the entrepreneurial world or why it had such a pull for me. I had no one I could bounce ideas off of, talk to about my challenges, or turn to for advice. Sure, I could read books on business and marketing, and I did, but the live, objective feedback I needed was sorely missing.

If there is one regret I have above all others, it is that I didn't join or form a Mastermind Group sooner.

I think back on the frustrations, wasted time, and money spent trying out ideas, starting new businesses, and attempting to make things work, and it pains me. It pains me because the bulk of it probably could have been avoided. I would be so much farther ahead than I am now if I had just thought to jump the learning curve by leveraging the ideas of others.

In business, there is absolutely no reason to reinvent the wheel. While it is true that the business landscape changes over time and new ideas and ways of doing things are always being brought to the forefront, it is also true that there are principles to be followed that will lead you to success. There's an old saying in the business world that "success leaves footprints." The trick is to understand these principles and then adapt them to your unique circumstances. In other words, just follow the footprints.

There is no better way to do that, in my opinion, than through a Mastermind Group.

ENJOY THE JOURNEY

Ralph Waldo Emerson once said, "Life is a journey, not a destination."

I remember not long ago picturing myself as an old man, eighty-three or eighty-four, and looking at myself in the mirror. I asked myself, "How did you change the world?" I remember being terrified of not having a satisfactory answer to that question. Based on that, I have redefined the word success to mean being happy with that answer when the dusk of life befalls me.

The only way, though, that I can be happy with that answer is to enjoy the journey every step of the way.

I have come to realize that, although in business it is the outcome—the results—that matter most, true joy and happiness in not just business, but in life that comes from enjoying the journey.

I have focused the bulk of this book on the specific outcomes and benefits that come from joining a Mastermind Group. However, I urge you not to start one or join one solely for those reasons. See the positive outcomes and the benefits gained that joining a Mastermind Group affords you as a little side bonus, as the icing on the cake.

The true joy you will experience as an entrepreneur is the adventure you embark upon each day of your life as you roll up your sleeves and get to work. The triumphs, the disappointments, the awesome wins, and the spectacular failures . . . these are things each of us experience at some point in our career. Being able to share that with a dedicated group of smart, savvy, business owners is beyond compare. That, my friend, is the stuff life is made of!

Whatever your reasons for wanting to start a Mastermind Group are, whether for money or because you just want to grow your own business, start it now. This week. Don't procrastinate it until the "time is right."

There's no such thing as the right time anyway. That's just an illusion. There will always be a million reasons for not starting your Mastermind Group and why right now isn't a good time. Don't make the same mistake I did and wait ten years before acting on it. Start now.

Remember the words of Goethe, "Whatever you can do, or dream you can do, begin it. Boldness has genius, power, and magic in it. Begin it now."

ABOUT THE AUTHOR

Tobe Brockner has been an entrepreneur his whole life, starting his first business as a baseball trading-card broker in the second grade. After graduating Boise State University, he started a marketing and advertising business that serves small business owners and teaches them how to market their products and services better. As a result of these relationships, Tobe has created and runs several local Mastermind Groups.

In his free time, Tobe enjoys reading, writing, and spending time with his two children, Beau and Scarlett. He and his wife, Kirsten, make their home just outside of Boise. You can learn more about Tobe and follow his blog at www. TobeBrockner.com.

READY TO START YOUR MASTERMIND GROUP, BUT WANT A LITTLE MORE GUIDANCE?

Now that you've finished *Mastermind Group Blueprint*, it's time to go deeper.

Introducing the

MASTERMIND GROUP
TOOLKIT

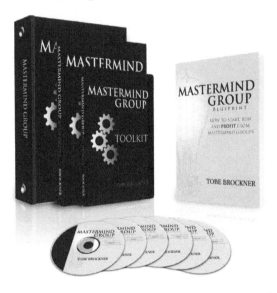

In this step-by-step tutorial, Tobe will personally train you in the process of getting your Group up and running in the shortest amount of time possible, sharing with you exactly what he did—and how you can do the same.

With the Mastermind Group Toolkit you will get everything you need—training, checklists, sample agreements, and more—to get you on the path to explosively growing your business through the power of masterminds.

GET STARTED NOW AT:

WWW.MASTERMINDGROUPTOOLKIT.COM